Praise for More than a Millionaire

"Randy Thurman takes you from where you are today and shows you in significant detail how to get out of debt, spend wisely, save, invest, and make better financial decisions. This book will help anyone see where their financial strengths and weaknesses are and what to do about it. I thoroughly enjoyed Thurman's writing style and advice for taking charge of your financial situation."

–Kevin Hogan, Psy.D., author of
The 12 Success Factors and *The Science of Influence*

"Randy Thurman has written a masterpiece on how to overcome financial obstacles, take smart risks, and invest in such a manner that wealth is created to become financially independent. I've known Randy for years and he is one of the most respected strategic thinkers and investors anywhere!"

–Stan Toler, author of *The Power of Your Attitude:
7 Choices for a Happy and Successful Life*

"Every great athlete relies on sound athletic fundamentals. The principles Randy teaches in *More than a Millionaire* are the fundamentals of sound financial planning. This book helps start you on a path to a brighter future."

–Guard Young, gymnast, Olympic Silver Medalist

"Randy Thurman's book *More than a Millionaire* is a down-to-earth book on seeing your financial life as more than just a net worth statement. It's about what's right for you. Randy demonstrates that your personal vision for 'financial independence' is just that—based on your definition, not someone else's. His approach is not complicated. It's easy to understand, and it will help you discover how to be More than a Millionaire."

–Doug Peterson, inspirational speaker and award-winning author of *Inspire Today's Journey: A Life Affirming Message for Each Day of Your Journey*

"As someone who works full time in men's ministry, one of the most common issues I see in men and in their families is a lack of knowledge about financial stewardship. I cannot thank Randy enough for his new book, *More than a Millionaire*. I believe it's going to not only educate men and women around the world, but also help them have the confidence to start winning again at building their financial futures. This book blessed my life tremendously. I highly recommend it."

–Cody Bobay, founder of Soulcon Ministries, author of *Soulcon Challenge*

MORE THAN A MILLIONAIRE

Also by Randy L. Thurman:

The All-Weather Retirement Portfolio: Your post-retirement guide to a worry-free income for life

One More Step: The 638 Best Quotes for the Runner

Get Rich Slowly...but Surely!

MORE THAN A MILLIONAIRE

YOUR PATH TO
WEALTH, HAPPINESS, AND A
PURPOSEFUL LIFE—STARTING NOW!

RANDY L. THURMAN, CFP®, CPA/PFS

Master Key
Publications

Published by

Master Key Publications,

Oklahoma City, Oklahoma

Interior design and typeset by Jan Allegretti

Cover design by Damonza

ISBN-13: 978-1-948607-00-1
ISBN-10: 1-948607-00-X

Master Key Publications, Oklahoma City, Oklahoma

This book is for educational and informational purposes only, and is not intended to provide assurances or guarantees of success; neither do the strategies contained herein represent personal recommendations for any reader. The reader is encouraged to consult a competent financial advisor to address his or her individual needs.

Links to resources and services are provided solely for the reader's convenience, and their inclusion should not be considered an endorsement of any resources, services, or products.

Information in this book is obtained from sources deemed to be reliable, but neither the author nor publisher warrant or guarantee the timeliness or accuracy of this information, nor shall they be liable for any errors or inaccuracies, regardless of cause. The information is believed to be factual and up to date, but it should not be regarded as a complete analysis of the subject. The recommendations and opinions stated are subject to change without notice.

Information in this book is not an offer to buy or sell or a solicitation of any offer to buy or sell any securities mentioned.

Past performance may not be indicative of future results, therefore the reader should not assume that future performance of any specific investment or strategy will be profitable or perform similarly in the future.

Different investment types carry different kinds of risk, therefore it should be noted that any specific investment or class of investment may or may not be suitable for any particular person or portfolio.

Historical performance of investment indexes and classes generally do not reflect the deduction of transaction fees, advisory fees, and/or custodial charges, which decrease overall performance. Economic factors, market conditions, and investment strategies impact any portfolio, resulting in a portfolio that may not match a particular benchmark.

I do not endorse or recommend the services of any investment advisor and/or brokerage company. Any given investment advisor and/or brokerage company is solely responsible for its services.

To Levi, my son.

I hope you find this book instructive and inspirational.

Enjoy life, prepare for the future, and never stop learning.

Love you, Son.

ACKNOWLEDGEMENTS

There are many who played a part in the making of this book...from helping me be a better writer, to educating me in the world of investing, to encouraging me to continue when I was ready to stop.

My wife, Pati. The most positive, upbeat, and energetic person I know, who loves me in spite of all my shortcomings.

Jan Allegretti. My editor and quiet inspiration. She is passionate about her editing and her causes. Without her, this book would not have been possible or, for that matter, readable.

Mom. I wouldn't be here if it wasn't for her constant encouragement. She was also a great second editor on the material. She got me my first library card well before I went to kindergarten and instilled the love of reading in me.

Heather Misialek. My personal assistant and all-time amazing person. Oftentimes she knows what I am about to think, before I think it. My work and personal life are better because of her. Thank you, Heather!

Carol Ringrose Alexander. An outstanding advisor at our firm who, through the years, has worked with me on my writing using her extensive writing experience.

Andrew Flinton. One of the most brilliant young minds in the field today and an advisor at our firm. I bounced many concepts off of him and received great suggestions.

Brenda Bolander. Our compliance officer at our firm who read through the manuscript for regulatory issues. She is also another outstanding advisor in our firm.

Jimmy J. Williams. The author of the foreword of my book *The All Weather Retirement Portfolio* and co-speaker with me at many AICPA Advanced Personal Financial Planning Conferences. I helped Jimmy get started in the business and then he helped me get better.

Clients. My clients over the last 30 years who encouraged me and trusted me with their life savings.

TABLE OF CONTENTS

Part IV
Make It Happen

INTRODUCTION

I guess you could say I learned the hard way. At least that's how my first lessons in finance came about. My brother and I grew up on a farm milking cows and raising pigs in Harrah, Oklahoma. Some kids had an allowance. We didn't—we had chores. If we needed something, we asked. Sometimes we got it, sometimes we didn't.

When it came time to go to college, I worked hard and paid my own way with the help of some hefty student loans. I got a decent job right out of grad school, working as a trainee in bank management. Unfortunately, my first year's salary was roughly equal to my student loan debt. I guess that wasn't so bad, or wouldn't have been if I could have put every dollar I made toward it that first year. But even back then, I really liked to eat and have a roof over my head. I had no clear plan for how I was going to pay off that loan, and certainly didn't have any direction regarding a path to financial security. So it should come as no surprise when I say I made my share of mistakes.

I will say I already had a pretty good habit of putting something from every paycheck into a savings account. (I'd learned that trick from a book called *The Richest Man in Babylon*. It seemed like a pretty good idea at the time. I know now it one of the smartest things I could have done...but more about that later.) But that monthly loan payment made it tough to stick with any kind of saving plan—heck, there was barely enough left to pay rent and buy groceries. My financial plan was a little like the Aerosmith song "Dream On"...I barely knew where the money was coming from, and I certainly didn't know where it was going.

Somehow every penny I made disappeared just about the time my next paycheck came along—sometimes (okay, often) sooner. I didn't keep a budget, so I had no clue what I was spending my money on, which meant I had little chance of making any improvements. I didn't see how I'd ever get out of debt or get ahead. I also didn't think I could afford renter's insurance, so when my apartment flooded (a frozen water pipe froze, busted, then unfroze...yep, it was a mess) and my furniture and half my clothes were ruined, I found out it was a lot tougher to "afford" to replace everything on my own. It seemed like I was going in the wrong direction...because I was.

Eventually losses like that became too painful, and I got tired of living paycheck to paycheck. I decided to make more informed choices about how I spent what little money I had. I began keeping track of how I spent my money. I'm not sure if I was more shocked or embarrassed to learn how much of my modest paycheck was going toward things I didn't really care much about. (It turned out I'd been spending as much to go out to lunch almost every day with the gang from work as I paid for rent. That's just crazy!) It was a great eye opener, and I started to make some better choices about where my money was going.

But I still had hard lessons to learn.

I'll never forget the day I got a phone call from a stock broker with a hot tip. Shares in Kelly-Johnston Restaurants were about to go through the roof, he said. There was a franchise nearby, and I knew the place well. Great food, and everyone was eating there. The broker could tell I was interested, so he kept selling...and I kept listening. Now, by this time I was going to night school to get an accounting degree on top of my M.B.A., and was working toward being an Assistant Vice President at the bank. You would think I'd have known better. I thought I did. I asked the broker to send me the financial statements for Kelly Johnstons, and I analyzed them just like they'd taught me in grad school. They looked so good I invested half of my life savings, $3,000. In six months the stock was worthless. I cannot even begin to tell you how painful that was!

The broker then called and said he wanted to make it up to me. This time he told me about an oil company whose stock was about to take off. They'd just hit a well and no one knew about it, so we had to move fast. At that point I was making decisions based on raw emotion—or more precisely, desperation. "I've got to make up my losses," I told myself. I invested the other half of my life savings in a little known oil company called Plano Petroleum. I bought it at $40 a share. In two weeks it was down to $6 a share.

In about six months and two weeks, I had lost my life's savings. I had worked and scrimped and sacrificed for a lot of years to save that money, and it was gone in what seemed like a heartbeat. To add insult to injury, I realized the broker had made a nice commission check each time I'd invested with him; he made money regardless of how I did.

I made a decision: This would never happen to me again. I started reading everything I could get my hands on about investing and money management. I also took courses on investing, money management, and accounting. I took the Certified Financial Planner™ courses and earned my certification. I sat for the CPA exam (and passed it the first time). Some said I was obsessed. But you know what? I soaked up so much information from so many different sources that eventually I was able to sort the good advice from the bad. I did my own research, tested theories and hypotheses against the hard data about how various strategies for investing and money management actually performed over time. Little by little I developed an approach that works, even through some of the toughest times our economy has seen in nearly a century—and I've seen it work for countless clients.

My story has a nice happy ending. But remember, I started out by learning what doesn't work. I made all of the mistakes I've told you about here—and countless more, believe me—even though I had good intentions. I sincerely wanted to handle my money responsibly, and at the time I believed that was exactly what I was doing. But there were too many choices for how to spend it and how to invest, and too much advice from people who knew little more than I did back then, or who were more interested in making money themselves than in helping me. Without a clear strategy based on time-tested guidelines, it was all pretty much a guessing game.

I suspect you've found yourself in a similar situation. If I'm right, you're the reason I wrote this book. I'd like to save you from making the kinds of mistakes I did, and get you on the path to financial success right away—today. And as you'll discover in the pages of this book, the sooner you get started in the right direction, the sooner you'll arrive at your destination with a larger retirement fund than you'd have if you wait as long as I did to get smart about money.

But there's something else we need to bring into this conversation, and it's this: It's not just about the money. I know, that's not what you expect to hear from a finance guy like me. But it's true. Money really doesn't buy happiness, and you certainly don't have to sacrifice happiness to become wealthy. In fact, one can support and enhance the other. That's right—I believe your financial success depends on making it a priority to live your life with purpose, meaning, and joy. It's not just about becoming a millionaire. My goal is to help you become More than a Millionaire, so you can achieve everything you hope for in your personal life and as a member of your community, as well as in your financial life.

It all starts here. I've put together everything you need to make sound decisions that will put you on the road to financial freedom and the kind of personal fulfillment you deserve.

- We'll start with a simple tool to help you make smart choices about how you spend your money, so you can use it to buy the things that matter most to you—now and in the years ahead.

- I'll show you some powerful strategies for increasing your income while also creating a career that's more rewarding, that brings a greater sense of purpose to your life.

- I'll share proven strategies for investing your money in a way that will minimize your risk while offering you the best expected return—so one day you can retire comfortably if you want to, or work only if and when you want to.

- Through it all we'll keep an eye on the money-management strategies that will help you do the things you love to do, and nurture your relationships with your family, your friends, and your community.

I won't kid you—it takes time, and it takes discipline. Some of the choices you'll need to make are easier than others. But one thing I'm sure of is this: It's all worth it. It may seem like an insurmountable climb to get from where you are now to where you want to be. But I've done it and I've seen others do it, and I know you can do it to. There will be obstacles to overcome, and there will be a few setbacks along the way. But as long as you stick with the plan I've provided here and keep your eye on the goal, you will get there.

The key is to begin. Just start with a few small steps, and soon you'll begin to see signs of progress. Then one day you'll realize you're in better financial shape than you've ever been before. Before you know it you'll be well on your way to becoming More than Millionaire.

Let's go.

PART I

THE "MORE THAN A MILLIONAIRE" JOURNEY

Is It for You?

CHAPTER 1

WHICH MOUNTAINS WOULD YOU LIKE TO CLIMB?

Wealth...millionaire...financial independence...rich guy. There's no shortage of words and phrases that get tossed around in the media and casual conversation when we talk about having lots of money. *Plenty* of money, I mean, enough to do all the things you dream about doing.

But what do all those words really mean? What exactly are your dreams? Which ones light you up the most? And how much would it take to make them a reality?

How much money is "enough"?

While we're at it, is money all it takes for you to live the life of your dreams, or will it require something more?

Before we dig into the pages of a book about becoming More than a Millionaire—and certainly before you take your first steps in that direction—let's stop and define our terms. Let's make sure you and I are talking about the same goals...the same dreams.

Financial independence. I'm guessing it's a safe assumption that one of your dreams is to be done worrying about money. First and foremost, you'd probably like to have the security of knowing you'll be able to pay your bills, without needing to stretch your last dollars just to make it to the end of the month. Beyond that, I imagine there have been days when you wished you didn't have to be tied to your job, that you could cut the cord and spend your days on your own terms, doing the things that bring you the most happiness. Maybe that means backpacking into the wilderness whenever you get the urge, or traveling, or playing golf or tennis every day. Or maybe it means doing work you love...or doing the work you already do, but with the freedom to cut loose and be as creative with it as you want to be.

Whatever it means for you, becoming financially independent would allow you to live a lifestyle that brings you enjoyment and that has meaning, without the *need* to work. If you continued to work, you'd do it because you want to, not because you have to. It would also give you the time and energy—*as well as* the money—to be there for friends, family, people you care about, and even your community, to support them with your talent and your treasure.

Millionaire. The word seems straightforward enough, but it's actually something of a moving target. It's often used, incorrectly, in reference to someone who earns $1 million or more in a year, or in one fortunate blast (think lottery, game show winner, an inheritance, or maybe a fat advance on that book you've been planning to write).

The textbook definition of "millionaire" is someone who has a net worth of $1 million or more. Add up the value of everything you own (sometimes called "assets"), including money in the bank, any investments you have, the equity in your home if you own it, and any property like a car, jewelry, even your stereo equipment. Then add up everything you owe (sometimes called "liabilities")—yes, everything, the loan on your car, your mortgage, school loans, and definitely any and all credit card balances. Subtract what you owe from what you own. That's your net worth.

I know you've just run a rough guestimate in your head, so...how'd you do? Not quite at that $1 million mark yet, right? Is it a negative number? Don't worry. That's why you're here. You can fix it.

More than a Millionaire. No, I'm not just talking about having $1.2 million, or even $2 million or more. That'd be fine, but there's more to it than the dollar value of your net worth. It's about a quality of life that can't be measured by running numbers on a calculator. It can't even be measured by looking at the balance in your investment accounts.

Being More than a Millionaire means you've cultivated a lifestyle that's about giving back, as much or more than it is about accumulating money. Does that surprise you? After all, I'm a financial advisor. My job description is about helping people make money. The thing is, I've been at this long enough to know that just building up a hefty investment account doesn't, by itself, make for a happy or meaningful life. I've learned from my own experience and from working with clients for some thirty years that the real prize is in what you can do with that money—for yourself, for your family, and for the people and things that matter to you.

Having a net worth of $1 million is not enough. Having $1 million in your retirement accounts isn't even enough. It's great to aim for milestones like those, and that's one part of what we're here for. But there's more. My wish for you is that you *also* have a rich, rewarding personal and professional life, and that you develop the habit of giving back to individuals, to your community, and to society at large...all of which will contribute to your personal happiness.

That's what being More than a Millionaire is all about. And that's where this journey will take you, if you let me show you how to get there. And, of course, if you're sure that's where you want to go.

Is it?

CHAPTER 2

 IS IT THE RIGHT PATH FOR YOU?

It may seem like a no-brainer that you want to be rich. Heck, everyone wants that, right?

Maybe…or maybe not. For a lot of people, once you dig a little deeper it becomes clear that it's more complicated than that. It's no secret that money, and how much you do or don't have, is a sensitive topic. Maybe it's human nature or maybe it's a cultural thing, but we seem to have a tendency to attach all kinds of hopes, worries, assumptions, judgments, and anxieties to it.

- If I had more money I'd be happy.
- If I had more money I'd be able to find the love of my life and get married.
- If I had more money I wouldn't have any worries.
- What if I get sick and can't work—how will I take care of my family?
- I'm stuck in a cycle of debt and deprivation, and I'll never get out of it.

- The rich get richer and the poor get poorer.
- The only way to become wealthy is to be a workaholic—no personal life, no social life, no fun.
- The only way to become wealthy is to trample on other people.
- The only way to become wealthy is to work at a high-paying job you hate, and keep doing it until you retire or die, whichever comes first.
- There's no way I want to be part of the 1%. The wealthy should be sharing their money with the other 99% of the population.
- It's always two steps forward, three steps back—every time I start to get ahead, some financial crisis comes along to eat up my savings and then some.
- I know I'll be financially secure someday. I have no idea how I'll get there—but I'm sure it will happen.

Let me say, right here and now, that to my way of thinking all of the above statements are false—that is, unless you buy into them. But, like I said, it's complicated. So much of the way we think about money and treat the money we have—or wish we had—is based on emotions, myths, and false assumptions. Why? Because too often that's what's been drummed into us since we were kids, and what we see playing out everywhere from advertising media and movie scripts to political campaigns.

Sometimes those ideas and assumptions become self-fulfilling prophecies. You may want to become wealthy, and feel prepared to work hard and apply the best strategies available. But if deep down you believe that wealthy people are greedy and selfish, chances are you'll sabotage your efforts in some way. I've seen it happen. Or perhaps the only wealthy person in your family became that way by working ninety-hour weeks until the day he retired, only to find himself with no one and nothing but a lot of regrets to keep him company during his retirement years. Seeing him now, you're convinced it's better to be poor and happy than wealthy and lonely.

I promise you, those aren't your only options. But if you believe they are, those beliefs carry a lot of power over your life and, whether you realize it or not, they can have a profound impact on the choices you make. The only way to break free of those powerful underlying messages is to hold them up to the light of day, understand what's going on, and choose to relate to money in a more productive, rational way.

It's also true that some people choose not to pursue wealth for perfectly legitimate reasons. Each of us is entitled to hold a unique view of the world, and to choose how we move through it, how we organize our lives, what we set as our priorities. Even as a financial advisor I can acknowledge the validity of choosing to forego the pursuit of wealth in favor of other priorities; it's entirely possible to lead a life that has value and significance without aspiring to or attaining wealth. As we all know, Mother Theresa lived a perfectly rewarding and profoundly significant life in abject poverty, caring for people in desperate need of help. Few would deny that her life had meaning and purpose, and more value than most people can ever aspire to no matter how much money they have. Clearly she made the choice that was right for her.

Maybe a similar choice is right for you as well, or maybe it's decidedly not. Or maybe your path is something closer to the middle of the road. What's most important at this stage of your financial journey is to become aware of what your own beliefs and values are, so you can choose the path that makes sense for you and eliminate any self-sabotaging negative judgments. One of the main things you'll gain from this book is a way out of any emotional, destructive relationship you may have to money, so you can use logic, good sense, and tried-and-true strategies to be financially successful—if that's what you really want.

If you're not sure the path to wealth is for you, I'd rather see you figure that out sooner than later. It's my experience that virtually anyone can become wealthy if he or she chooses to. But it takes patience, discipline, hard work, and some degree of sacrifice to get there. None of that makes sense if it's not your destination of choice.

If you decide that it is, knowing exactly *why* you're doing it will help you stay motivated when you'd like to blow a wad of cash on a new sound system for your car or a vacation you can't quite afford, or when life hands you one of its financial setbacks. Trust me, there will be times when the going gets tough, no matter how resolute you are about building your financial future. Remembering why you're doing it will help carry you through those times.

SHOULD YOU?

Before we go any further, let's take a step back and ask the one question that matters most as you prepare to set out on the path to become More than a Millionaire: Should you even bother? If you haven't started saving yet, have you ever wondered why?

Is it selfish to "wanna be rich"?

Negative judgments about money are common, and can be a powerful influence on your choices. They can also undermine your efforts to save, even if you're not aware you have them. So let's start by examining some of the negative beliefs that might hold you back.

- **The notion that nice people don't become wealthy**, or that it's necessary to undermine the success of others to attain wealth for yourself
- **The belief that desiring wealth is inherently selfish or greedy**, which causes feelings of guilt when you think about making it a priority in your life
- **A "zero sum" view of wealth** vs. a view that encompasses abundance for all. What right do you have to accumulate all that money when people all around the world are starving?

Negative judgments about wealth are common in our culture, and in some circles they're drummed into us from an early age. Because they can be related to your core belief system, they can have a very powerful influence on your life, whether you realize it or not. Core beliefs operate on a subconscious level, so they can lead you to make choices for reasons you're not even aware of. If you believe that you must be greedy to do well, or that to do well financially is wrong for whatever reason, you will find a way to sabotage your efforts to become More than a Millionaire. With so much at stake, let's take a closer look at those deeply rooted beliefs, and see how they hold up in the light of day.

First and foremost, it is absolutely not necessary to do harm to anyone or anything in order to become wealthy. There's no need to take money that should have gone to someone else, or to undermine someone else's success to ensure yours. It's true enough that there are people in the world who have accumulated wealth by stepping on others. But you don't have to be that person. In fact, it's my experience that the more you lift others up, the more likely you are to find success yourself. For starters, it's just good business practice to treat others well. When you do, your boss will support your career, your customers will buy more products from you, other people will respect you enough to open doors and throw opportunities your way. But there's more to it than that. Call it karma, call it "what goes around comes around," or just the laws of nature—whatever it is, life tends to reward people who are honest, generous, and kind. In fact, being a good person is high on my list of requirements for becoming More than a Millionaire.

But maybe your concern has more to do with the notion that wanting to become wealthy is inherently greedy. Perhaps you were raised with the idea that living a simple lifestyle is an indication of moral character. Maybe you even feel you'd be embarrassed to drive around in a fancy car, as though you were trying to flaunt your wealth. Those are valid viewpoints if they resonate for you and you consciously choose to embrace them.

But let's be clear about one thing: Being financially secure doesn't necessarily mean you have to own a lot of fancy stuff, let alone flaunt it. At the same time, there's nothing wrong with owning nice things, or even expensive things. It's about balance, and having the freedom to make choices that feel right and that bring you happiness. I'm a fan of being reasonably frugal. At the same time, I think it's fine to enjoy the money you have, as long as you stay on track to meet your long-term financial goals. When you're financially successful you can buy the fanciest car you can afford, if that brings you pleasure. But if you're more comfortable buying and consuming less—making a small footprint, as they say—you can do that no matter how much money is in your investment account.

Even if you do choose to own the best and brightest trinkets and gadgets your money can buy, your success does not diminish anyone else, or undermine anyone else's opportunity to be equally successful, or more so. To believe it does is to believe in what we call a "zero-sum economy," or the notion that if one person or organization or society gains, another one loses. A game of chess is a zero sum game—there's one winner and one loser. But money doesn't work like that. On the contrary, money tends to generate more money, so that one person's success is a catalyst for the success of others.

There are simple, real-world examples of this all around you. Think about a successful business in your home town. Maybe there's a great Italian restaurant downtown, and it's always packed during the dinner hour, especially on weekends. Business is good, so the owners enjoy the benefits of an excellent income. They also keep a full staff of cooks, servers, dishwashers, and a couple of bookkeepers employed year round. And because the business is so successful, everyone earns an above-average wage for the work he or she does. Each of those employees in turn makes enough money to take good care of her family, and spend a little extra when she goes out on her night off. That means she spends money supporting other local businesses, which in turn become successful, pay their employees well...and so it goes.

Your wealth, if you choose to attain it, does more to lift others up than your poverty ever will. When you have more money you can spend more money. Even more important is that when you have money, you can do good things for others that you can't do when you're poor. You can make cash donations to charitable organizations, pay for your kids' college education, or look after your dad in his elder years if he didn't become More than a Millionaire himself. Eventually it will buy you the freedom to work only when, if, and how you want to, so you can devote your time and energy to making memories with your family and giving back to your community.

Call me crazy, but I sure don't see anything greedy about that. Do you?

Best I can tell, money is morally neutral. It's how you accumulated it, what you become in the process, and what you do with it that counts.

But is it really worth it?

Even if you don't carry any moral judgments about money, maybe your concerns are more about logistics, or about your quality of life while you're in the process of building wealth. It's understandable that you'd have questions about that. So let's take a closer look at those concerns as well.

- **You want to enjoy life now.** Why save all your money to enjoy later, when "later" may never come? What if you make a wealthy retirement your goal, but you don't live long enough to retire?

- **The kind of work you want to do just doesn't pay well enough to build a wealthy future.** You work in a non-profit, or in an industry that characteristically pays substandard wages. Maybe you're an artist who doesn't want monetary goals to interfere with your creative freedom.

- **You want the freedom and flexibility to live your life on your terms,** and don't want to be tied to a job for forty hours a week, fifty weeks a year. Whether it's about spending quality time with your family, having the freedom to travel on a regular basis, or just a desire to live an unstructured life that isn't governed by someone else's schedule, you're a free spirit...an independent soul. A typical nine-to-five job just isn't for you.

- **You're convinced it's just not worth the effort and sacrifice—and probably not even possible to build up**

any significant amount of savings. Everything keeps getting more expensive, and you just don't see a way to do more than live paycheck to paycheck.

All of these are legitimate reasons to question whether becoming More than a Millionaire is the right path for you. But in my opinion, they're all based on a rather limited view of how money works or about your options regarding jobs and income. If I may, I'd like to offer a broader and brighter perspective. Since your financial future depends on it, it's worth a look...yes?

Let me begin by sharing a story about someone who defied many common assumptions about what it takes to become wealthy. Earl Crawley spent his entire career working as a parking lot attendant for the Mercantile Bank in Baltimore. After 44 years his yearly salary was just $20,000. Even so, he'd managed to accumulate investments worth more than $500,000. How did he do it? Well, he worked some odd jobs here and there, mowing lawns or washing windows, and applied the extra cash to his savings accounts. But mostly he did it by being careful about what he spent—and by saving on a regular basis, even if the amount he saved was a pittance by most standards. He invested carefully (he bought one share of IBM stock back in 1981), and asked questions and listened carefully to advice offered by the brokers and financial advisors he saw every day in his parking lot. He now coaches other budding investors through an investment club he started at his church.[1]

---

[1] Peter Anderson, "Retiring Wealthy on an Average Salary: The Story of the Persevering Parking Attendant," Smart on Money: Making Smart Decisions

Here's the thing…actually, several things.

- You don't have to make a lot of money to build a sizable retirement account.
- You don't have to slave away at a high-powered job you hate, just so you can pull down a high-powered income.
- You don't have to study finance or spend your weekends poring over the *Wall Street Journal* to figure out how to secure your financial future.
- Becoming More than a Millionaire doesn't have to rule your life.

What it does require is commitment, and a well-planned strategy that you can implement now, that will grow with you as your life evolves and your circumstances change, and that you can stick with for years to come. The strategy is simple enough. I've outlined the details in the pages of this book. The commitment, of course, has to come from you, and is only sustainable if you keep your eye on the prize—and if the prize is one you really want.

Do you really want to become More than a Millionaire? If you say no, this book is not for you. If your response is an emphatic "Yes!" and especially if it's "I'm still not sure," then let's dig a little deeper to find out what kind of future you'd like to create for yourself.

---

about Your Money, http://www.smartonmoney.com/retiring-wealthy-on-an-average-salary-the-story-of-the-persevering-parking-attendant/, accessed November 18, 2016.

Discover Your Reasons Why

Becoming wealthy requires discipline—ongoing discipline, over a period of many years, in fact for most of your life. It even requires some sacrifice, particularly in the early years. But so do other things, maybe even most other things that matter to you. In a sense, we all make trade-offs every day, whether we realize it or not. Often it comes down to choosing between a short-lived pleasure now or a more lasting benefit later, or foregoing something we want so we can have something else we want more. Each choice you make as you go through your day takes you closer to an end result. But if you don't have a particular end result in mind—one you consciously choose— 30 years from now you may find that you've ended up in a place you never wanted to go.

Whatever path you choose, it makes sense to decide sooner rather than later what you value, what matters to you, so you can be sure the small choices you make each and every day become small steps that eventually lead to the destination you really want. Maybe you're willing to sacrifice that trip to Italy this summer if it means you'll be able to spend your retirement years traveling around the world. Or maybe you value your freedom so much that you'd rather work as little as possible, even though it reduces the chance you'll ever be able to quit working completely. Either one is a valid choice. What's important is that you make a conscious choice, knowing full well what the trade-offs are—what you'd be sacrificing and what you'll gain as a result. If you're happy with the net result, then it's probably the right choice for you.

To help you do that, I've put together a list of questions that will help you explore your own values, your own goals, and your own priorities. Some of the questions may seem vague, but that's intentional—just see what they bring up for you and go with it. Start by going through the list quickly, and write down the first response that comes to mind. Then go back through the list more carefully and spend some time with each item, give it more thought, and weigh all the consequences of the choices you make for each question. Write down all of your responses as you go. Be honest with yourself—your answers are for you alone, so don't be afraid of anyone else's judgments. When you're finished, I think your "I'm still not sure" will have evolved into a better awareness of the life you really want to create for yourself, now and in the years to come. Most important, it will point you to a path that will take you there.

Self-exploration:

- What do you want from life?
- Do you feel an obligation to make a contribution to the world? If so, in what way?
- What's your ideal job?
- What are you willing to give up in order to have that ideal job?
- If you had more money than you could ever need, so you didn't have to work, how would you spend your days?
- If you have a family, or if you would like to have a family someday, what values regarding money would you like to impart to your children?

- Do you hope to retire one day? If so, when?
- Where would you like to live when or if you retire?
- What matters to you?
- What are you willing to sacrifice for? (A nice home, travel, time with your family, unstructured time, freedom to choose how you spend your time, time to advocate for causes you care about, freedom to choose where you live and what kind of home you have....)
- What are you unwilling to compromise on?
- What were you doing the last time you lost track of time?
- What makes you feel a sense of purpose?
- Write the story of the rest of your life, as you would like it to unfold. (Be as brief or as detailed as you like, but don't hesitate to write a truly thrilling life story. Go ahead...create your masterpiece!)

All of these questions are designed to help you identify what's important to you, what your priorities are. Keeping those priorities and values in mind will help you identify the goals that are appropriate for you, and also help you sustain the discipline and commitment it takes to achieve those goals, whatever they may be. With all of that in place, you'll have a clearer sense of where you want to go, so you can make the choices that will get you there.

Identify Your Vision for Your Future

Where do you want to go? What direction do you want your life to take? Will becoming More than a Millionaire help you get there?

There's pretty good evidence to suggest our thoughts create reality. What you imagine will happen often does—more often than you might think. That's where those underlying beliefs about money can come into play. If you expect to be poor for the rest of your life...be careful, you just might make it happen. On the other hand, if you envision for yourself a life that's rich with material, emotional, and spiritual rewards—and imagine it in as much detail as possible—you'll give yourself a leg up in that direction.

So...what's your vision for your life?

Before you answer that question, let's take a look at a few possible scenarios for your future. Some might resemble the life you want, others might look more like the life you feel doomed to live. Try each one on for size and see what you think.

Scenario #1.

Your net worth is more than a million dollars. Financially you've made it. You have fought and clawed your way to the top, leaving a wake of destruction in your path. No one in your family loves or even likes you, but, "Who cares," you say, "they're deadbeats anyway." None of them has as much money as you, so what they think of you doesn't matter.

You don't see your family much because you're always working. If you do go to a social engagement it's with a business partner or client. Your significant other has his or her own activities and social life, and it seems you spend less and less time together with each passing year. You never take a vacation because vacations cost money and, anyway, who needs them and who has the time? You don't have time to exercise because you're always working. Yes, you're about a hundred pounds overweight, but food is one of your few pleasures in life. What the heck, you've earned the right to indulge yourself.

You hate what you do for a living, but it pays good money. You are the boss, and don't those peons who work for you know it. You don't have ulcers, but you do cause them. Your motto is, "Look after number one," and you live by it. You'll probably work until the day you drop, because...what else is there to do?

Scenario #2.

You are retired and living on Social Security. You barely make ends meet, but your children help out as much as they can. Sometimes you feel like a burden to your family, but they don't seem to mind. You had a great time in life, spent your money when you had it and enjoyed yourself. But your Social Security check doesn't go very far, so you can no longer do the kinds of things you used to do. Your options are pretty limited.

You're close to your family because you always made it a priority to spend time with them, even if it meant turning down jobs that would have advanced your career. Your youngest son was in a car accident recently and ran up some hefty bills. You wish you could help him out financially, but you simply can't. You have many friends, and many of them are struggling financially, as you are. You'd like to be able to throw a few extra dollars their way, too, but there just aren't any extra dollars to share.

You wish you had started saving for these senior years when you were young, but it never seemed like the right time—there was always something else to do with any extra cash you had in your pocket. Sometimes it was a necessary expense, other times it was an indulgence you really enjoyed. Eventually it was just too late.

Scenario #3.

You have lived a balanced life. You worked hard, but you also took care of the other things that mattered to you. You have a great relationship with your family and a strong circle of friends who love and respect you. You've always taken care of yourself, as well. You try to eat right (well, most of the time) and make it a point to get out and move a little every day. It makes you feel good about yourself, and besides, you know you won't be much good to anyone else if you're not feeling your best

You started saving and investing when you were in your late twenties, and now you're about ready to retire. You have a lot of options available to you, with a retirement fund that will allow you to live where you want to live, travel a bit, and even treat your kids and their families to a nice vacation now and then. You're looking forward to spending more time volunteering as a Big Brother, mentoring young boys who come from broken families. You recently donated funds to the local YMCA to help them build a new rec center. And boy, do the kids love it!

It's true enough that life has its challenges. It always does. But it's a lot easier to meet those challenges when you have the financial means to pay unexpected expenses, hire the right professional, or buy a bigger Band-Aid, so to speak.

All in all, life is good, and you strive to continue to make it so. Your motto is, "Every day is a good day, and if you don't think so, try missing one."

Here's my vision for a good life—the operative word being "my." Yours may be similar or it may be very different, and that's fine. The point here is to explore different possibilities to help you arrive at your own vision. Toward that end, here's a vision I believe is worthwhile:

You have more than $1 million in your retirement account, which you've accumulated without sacrificing your values. You are debt free. You contribute a portion of your time and money to charity on a regular basis. You work because you choose to, not because you have to, and you're respected by your colleagues. You work and volunteer because both bring you joy, and let you feel you're making a positive difference in people's lives. You have a close personal relationship with family members and can help them out with your time, talent, and treasure when appropriate. You are in great physical shape and work out several times a week. Your spiritual life is fulfilling. You use your wealth to create fond memories and lead a good life.

What's your vision?

Now it's your turn. What does your ideal life look like? Describe it in detail, and be sure to include all the aspects of your life that matter to you—work, play, family, community, and anything else you care about.

[Please take a few moments, or longer,
to write your vision for a good life.]

How do you feel when you imagine yourself living that life? Does it make your heart race just a little...or a lot? If I told you that you could create that life for yourself, would you be willing to work toward it? Would you be willing to apply self-discipline and commitment to make it a reality?

I'm here to tell you that you can in fact create that life for yourself, and within the pages of this book I'll tell you exactly how to do it—how to organize your finances, set your goals, and take the necessary steps to achieve them. I'm not saying it'll be easy, or that it will happen overnight. It takes discipline and dedication, and a commitment over the course of many years to stick with the plan I'll lay out for you. But you *can* make it happen.

So the question is this: Is it worth it to you? If you could start today building the life you described in your vision for your future, would you be willing to work toward making it happen? Do you want to become More than a Millionaire?

If the answer is, "Yes," then turn the page and let's get started.

CHAPTER 3

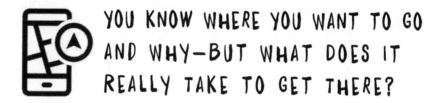 YOU KNOW WHERE YOU WANT TO GO AND WHY—BUT WHAT DOES IT REALLY TAKE TO GET THERE?

Now that we have some good clarity now about what it really means to become More than a Millionaire, and the reasons you've decided to make it a priority in your life, it's time to explore what it takes to get there. As I suspect you've discovered, there are more books and articles and websites devoted to the topic than you can shake a stick at. Everyone and his brother seem to have an angle on how you can find your way to financial freedom. Most of them lead with a pitch for how easy it can be, or how fast you can get there, or how you can become wealthy without incurring any risk. And why not? We'd all choose fast, easy, and safe over slow, difficult, and risky, every time—assuming, of course, that the strategy actually worked.

The problem is, most so-called financial gurus are making a splash by promoting the latest, greatest idea about how to build wealth, without applying the most fundamental principles of how money actually works in the real world. And if you choose a path that doesn't actually take you where you want to go, you may find out too late that your path to retirement is actually a dead end.

DETOURS—OR DEAD ENDS?

With that in mind, let's do a reality check to examine the various options you've likely read or heard or thought about, and make sure you choose a proven, workable, realistic plan...a route to financial freedom that will actually take you to your intended destination.

Get Rich the Quick and Easy Way

There are plenty of offers, ads, pitches, and blogs that profess to show you how to get rich quickly and easily—the four-hour work week, the online business that will generate income while you play golf, the computer program that will tell you when to buy and sell stocks as a sure-fire way to win on the stock market. Unfortunately, those "quick and easy" plans don't work.

It's true enough that someone, somewhere, sometime may actually have been lucky enough to strike it rich using one or another of those get-rich-quick schemes. But does that one-off success offer any assurance that you'll be able to replicate it? Think about it: If there was a sure-fire, fast and easy way to make a ton of money without lifting a finger or breaking a sweat, don't you think everyone would be doing it? Everyone *isn't* doing it, because there is no get-rich-quick strategy that you can count on to build the kind of financial security you need.

That doesn't mean there isn't a reliable way to create wealth. There is. But it takes time, patience, discipline, and diligence, along with a sound strategy for building wealth based on realistic, time-tested principles. It may not happen in the time frame you prefer. But it can and will happen—*if* you choose your strategy with care and implement it with discipline and consistency.

Do you want to stake your financial future on luck, or proven principles that work?

Safety First, a.k.a. No Risk and No Loss

Maybe you're the kind of person who likes to avoid worry at all cost. You want to play it safe, and eliminate any chance you could lose a dime of your hard-earned money. The ups and downs of the stock market make most investments sound like something akin to Russian roulette. From what you've seen, it just doesn't make sense to risk your financial future on something so volatile. The obvious solution is to put your retirement savings into something really secure like a savings account at a big bank, or maybe a CD at the credit union. Or is it?

It's true enough that the money you put into a savings account or CD is safe, in the sense that for every $10 you put into the account you'll get $10 (plus a little) back when it's time to retire. But what most people don't realize is that the $10 (plus a little) you take out probably won't buy as much as the $10 you put in. The number of dollars you have in the account may never go down, but the purchasing power of those dollars almost certainly will. Here's why.

There was a time when you could get 10% or 12% or more interest on a long-term CD at your local bank. Heck, in August of 1981, six-month CDs were paying a whopping 17.98%.[2] As it turned out, mortgages that month were running at 17.28%, and in September and October they soared above 18%,[3] so...as they say, there's no such thing as a free lunch.

For better or for worse, those days are gone. As I write this, the national average rate for the same six-month CD comes in at 0.13%.[4] Put $1,000 into one of those babies and after six months you'll have earned exactly $1.30. That's almost enough to buy yourself a cup of coffee—but only if you split the bill with a friend (and I'll prove it to you in a minute). Roll that CD over for the next 15 years and, assuming the interest rate doesn't change, you'll end up with a grand total of $1,020.[5] Your *total* net gain over that fifteen-year period would be just 2%. That's hardly what I'd call letting your money work hard for you...it's more like hardly workin'.

But there's more here to be sad about than just a dismal return on your investment. You've been on this planet long enough to see the cost of things you buy go up...and up...and up. In the year 2000

[2] "CD Interest Rate Chart," Forecastchart, http://www.forecast-chart.com/rate-cd-interest.html, accessed October 28, 2016.
[3] "30-Year Fixed-Rate Mortgages Since 1971," FreddieMac, http://www.freddiemac.com/pmms/pmms30.htm, accessed October 26, 2016.
[4] "Weekly National Rates and Rate Caps," Federal Deposit Insurance Corporation, https://www.fdic.gov/regulations/resources/rates/, accessed October 28, 2016.
[5] "Compound Interest Calculator - Savings Account Interest Calculator," Bankrate, http://www.bankrate.com/calculators/savings/compound-savings-calculator-tool.aspx, accessed October 28, 2016.

you could buy a first-class postage stamp for 34 cents.[6] In 2015 that stamp cost 49 cents, or 44% more. Are you a coffee drinker? If you were old enough to drink it in 2000, you would have paid roughly $1.96 for a cup. By 2015 the price was up to $2.70. That's a 38% increase in just fifteen years.

Now let's go back to that hypothetical CD you might have bought with your $1,000, and the 2% return it would earn over fifteen years. Do you see where I'm going with this...? Your investment returns a gain of 2% over fifteen years, but the cost of a cup of coffee or a postage stamp could increase by roughly 40% in fifteen years. Expand those numbers to cover everything you buy—and everything you might want to buy in your golden years—and you can see that you'll lose a whole lot of purchasing power if your return on investment doesn't keep up.

Let's be clear. The overall rate of inflation is dependent on many varied and complex factors beyond the price of coffee or postage stamps. It also fluctuates from year to year depending on a host of factors in the United States and global economies. But historically the cost of living has gone up, on average, between about 2% and 3% per year. (Of course, the average during your lifetime may ultimately be more or less than that. I think it's prudent, though, to let history be your guide.) As a case in point, between 2000 and 2015 the cost of living went up by 37.79%; the average annual increase during that time was 2.16%. That means you would have needed $1,377.90 in

6 "Cost of a first class U.S. postage stamp," Johnston's Archive, http://www.johnstonsarchive.net/other/postage.html, accessed October 28, 2016.

2015 to buy as much as your $1,000 would have bought in 2000.[7] Do you see why your CD with a compounded return of $1,020 actually gives you a *net loss* of purchasing power?

I'm all about protecting your investment from unnecessary risk of loss. I understand that putting your money in a protected savings account or CD *feels* like a way to eliminate your risk. But when you understand how money really works, you can see why "playing it safe" with a low-interest account will virtually ensure you lose purchasing power over time. The dollar amount of your investment may never go down, but the *value* of your dollars almost certainly will. On top of that, you lose the opportunity to earn a much higher rate of return than those savings vehicles can offer.

You—and your money—can do better.

Live for Today, Pay for It Later

You're young. You want to enjoy life. There are places to go, cars to buy, and maybe a certain lifestyle you'd like to enjoy. Every week, it seems, another offer for a credit card shows up in your mailbox, complete with an offer for cash back or 0% interest rate for the first year. There's even an option to refinance your home and take out an extra $10,000 or $20,000 or more against the equity on your house, with only a small increase in your monthly payment. Why not make the most of life now? What's so bad about living in the moment?

I'm not here to tell you what's good or bad or what's right or wrong. But I can tell you this: The only way to secure your financial

---

[7] "The Cost of Living Calculator," American Institute for Economic Research, https://www.aier.org/cost-living-calculator, accessed October 28, 2016.

future is to live within your means today. One of the greatest obstacles to building wealth is debt, because the interest you pay on that debt is like throwing money out the window each and every month. It's money you spend solely for the use of someone else's money, with absolutely no financial or long-term gain or benefit to you. Every dollar you pay in interest on debt is a dollar that, if you invest it instead, could be earning more dollars for you, which in turn could be earning even more dollars, to eventually buy your financial freedom.

So, I'd like to pose a question. If there's something you're considering buying now, but you can only buy it if you use someone else's money and go into debt, what's more important to you— making that purchase now, or getting one step closer to financial freedom? Would you rather take that fancy vacation or buy that luxury car today, or become More than a Millionaire tomorrow?

It really does come down to that. The interest you pay to someone else will strain your budget and drain your finances like a hole in the bottom of a swimming pool. It will also put a small—or not so small—knot in your stomach each time you have to write a check for something you stopped enjoying months or years ago. On the other hand, the peace of mind you get from knowing you're securing your future by living debt-free is far greater than the short-lived rush of having or buying something you can't afford.

If you're patient and disciplined, and take responsibility for your financial future today, the time will come when you will be able to buy the things you really want with your own money, without going into debt and jeopardizing your chance at financial freedom.

I promise you it's worth waiting for.

A Tried and True Path to Success

There is a road to wealth that works—not a quick and easy one, but one that takes time and discipline and a strategy that has been crafted and researched and fine-tuned and tested by someone who has been doing this for more than 30 years...that is, by me. No one can promise you a specific return on any particular investment portfolio, over any given length of time. What I can offer you is a comprehensive strategy for managing your money in a way that will put you on the road to success, and for investing that money in a way that offers you the best possible chance of a good expected rate of return, while minimizing your risk. I've been studying money and how it works for more than three decades, and I've combined my experience with that of countless other professionals to create a plan that will work for you.

How do I know it will work? Because I've tested it against reams of data covering decades of performance in the financial markets in the United States and around the world. I've seen these strategies work for more than a thousand clients I've served over the years, and watched it stand up to the worst financial climate since the Great Depression. While that's no guarantee of how the plan will perform in the future, I think you'll agree it's passed a pretty strong test.

That's the strategy for becoming More than a Millionaire that you'll learn in this book. If you're willing to take it step by step, take responsibility for what you earn and how you spend your money now, and apply my simple, time-tested approach to investing your money for the best possible expected return with a minimum level of risk, you will put yourself on the path to success.

PART II

GETTING STARTED

CHAPTER 4

YOUR ESSENTIAL FIRST STEPS

We've all heard it a hundred times: A journey of a thousand miles begins with a single step. It's true that, no matter what your goal is, you can't realize it unless you take that very first step, even if it's a small one. It's also true that it's better if that first step points you in the right direction. If it takes you closer to Canada when your goal is to hike to Mexico, at some point you'll have to backtrack to get back on course.

With that in mind, I can't overstate how important it is that you take a few well-planned steps now, at the beginning of your journey toward financial security. If you do, every step that follows will be a whole lot easier. You'll encounter fewer obstacles along the way and reach your goal much more quickly.

When that goal is to become More than a Millionaire, there are five steps you need to take at the very start that are critical to your success. They are:

1. Maintain a positive cash flow.

2. Manage debt wisely.

3. Find the right home.

4. Prepare for a rainy day.

5. Create a shelter against financial storms.

STEP 1: MAINTAIN A POSITIVE CASH FLOW

I once saw a cartoon that said, "Happiness is a positive cash flow." I don't think that's all it takes, but I do feel it's easier to be happy when you have more money coming in than going out. The odd part is that how much you make is less important than how much you save. Even if you make a million dollars a year, if you spend a million and one...I'm telling you, you're not going to become financially independent. Seems obvious, yes?

Then why is it so challenging for so many? I've had plenty of high-income people come in our door who spend more than they make. Many spend money they don't have, to buy things they don't need, just to impress people they don't care for. Crazy, right? So why do they do it? It's a good question, and finding the answer probably requires plumbing the depths of human psychology. For our purposes it's enough to recognize that, in the midst of trying to maintain a lifestyle that's beyond their means, those people lose sight of the larger—and far more important—goals they have for their lives.

I can promise you that your goal of becoming More than a Millionaire is relatively easy to attain if you're willing to take this one, simple first step: Spend less money than you make. Whether you hope to become financially independent, provide positive experiences for yourself and for people you care about, have the freedom and means to make a meaningful difference in the lives of others less fortunate than you, or all of the above, it all *starts with* maintaining a positive cash flow. You simply can't get ahead financially, *regardless of your income*, if you spend more than you make.

You can achieve it all. You must, however, take your first step in the right direction.

Step 2. Manage Debt Wisely

You've always wanted a serious in-home theatre. You've spotted an incredible one on sale for only $5,000. Wow—a setup like this would normally cost at least $7,000 or $8,000! You don't have the five grand, but you figure you can just put it on the credit card. The minimum payments on it will be a bit of a stretch, but manageable. Besides—look at all the money you'll save! You plunk down that card, set up your new system, and invite your friends over for an awesome night at the movies.

So how much do you think that shiny new system will end up costing you? And how long will it take to pay it off? Go ahead, give me your best guess. I'll wait.

Okay, now for the cold, hard truth.

Let's assume that, like most people, you unknowingly opted for one of the most expensive cards, one that offers cash back for purchases you make using the card. Many people like them because...hey, it's free money, isn't it? Your $5,000 purchase is rewarded with $75, or maybe even $100 back. You take your spouse or significant other on a long overdue dinner date on the credit card company. Life is good.

However, as I write this, the interest rate on a typical cash-back credit card is around 20.9%[8], and for a $5,000 purchase your starting minimum monthly payment would be around $200 (decreasing as you pay down the balance). So how long will it really take you to pay off that fancy new home theater? If you pay only the minimum payment, it will take you 146 months. That's more than twelve years. As fast as technology is changing these days, do you think that system will still seem fancy and new seven or eight years from now...or two?

And what about that great deal you got on the system? When all is said and done, you'll end up paying roughly $8,688.40.[9] And that's if you make all your payments on time. Miss a payment or two and you could be hit with a penalty interest rate up to 29.99% per year.[10] Suddenly that theater system looks more like a scary movie than a dream come true.

---

[8]"Average Credit Card Interest Rates," ValuePenguin, http://www.valuepenguin.com/average-credit-card-interest-rates, accessed June 21, 2016.
[9] "Credit card minimum payment calculator," Bankrate, http://www.bankrate.com/calculators/credit-cards/credit-card-minimum-payment.aspx, accessed June 13, 2016.
[10] "Average Credit Card Interest Rates," ValuePenguin, http://www.valuepenguin.com/average-credit-card-interest-rates, accessed June 13, 2016.

Let's look at a different option. Instead of buying that theater system, what if you put your monthly payment of $200 into a retirement plan, maybe your 401(k) at work, which not only *pays* you money (it pays a return on investment instead of charging you interest) but also has tax benefits. In the same 146 months it would take you to pay off the credit card bill, you can save about $2,867 off your annual taxes,[11] *and* accumulate roughly $16,000[12] more in your 401(k)—plus, if your company matches the money you put into your retirement plan, you'll accumulate substantially more.

This is just one quick glimpse into the impact of incurring debt rather than investing your money. Granted, there are less frivolous reasons to borrow money than the home theater scenario I've described here. Buying a home or a dependable car comes to mind. But usually when I see people who have problems in this area it's because of impulse buying, and a debt that carries the high interest rates typical of credit cards. That's a recipe for disaster where your finances are concerned. It's pretty darn tough to secure your financial future if you're paying hard-earned cash to some credit card company for the privilege of buying a new toy you can't really afford.

That's why one of the first essential steps toward becoming More than a Millionaire is to manage debt wisely, and with an only-

---

[11] Assuming you're in a 28% federal income tax bracket and a 5% state income tax bracket.

[12] I say "roughly" because returns are variable. This is a conservative estimate based on an average monthly investment over the same period of time, with the same total out-of-pocket cash outlay as you would have given to the credit card company.

when-absolutely-necessary mindset. Taking out a mortgage to buy a house has benefits that can outweigh the downside of debt. If your car breaks down and you don't have the cash to buy a new one, get a loan with the lowest interest rate you can find and buy the most modest car that will serve your purpose, then pay off the car loan as quickly as you can. If going back to school will help you land a job that will increase your income and let you do work that brings more meaning to your life, taking on a manageable amount of debt in the form of a school loan may be the right choice. Bottom line, go into debt only where necessary to buy basic necessities of life, or when it clearly takes you closer to realizing your long-term goals. Period, end of story.

If you're already upside down on credit cards, here's my suggestion: Take your credit cards and put them in a Ziploc bag. Fill the bag with water and put it in the freezer. You have now frozen your credit cards. (I know...I can see you rolling your eyes.) This will make impulse buying much harder. Now, budget as much as you can to reduce the debt. Check the expense guidelines in Chapter 5, "Your Spending Plan," for recommendations on how much to allocate to your credit cards. Then make the minimum monthly payment on all the cards except for the one with lowest balance, and put the rest of your budgeted amount into that one. That means you will pay it off faster, which will give you a nice dose of positive reinforcement. When that card is paid off, cut it up and start on the card with the next lowest balance. Repeat until all the cards are paid off.

One last bit of advice about those paid-in-full credit cards. I may surprise you on this one, but *do not* close those accounts. Keep the cards frozen away in those Ziploc bags so you don't use them, but keep the accounts active. Having unused credit accounts will translate to a higher credit score, because it demonstrates how good you are at managing money. That means you'll get a lower interest rate on a mortgage or car loan if and when you need one.

Speaking of that car loan, go ahead and get one if you need it. When you finish paying it off, continue making the monthly payment—but instead of paying on a loan, put the money into your own car fund, preferably a highly liquid, safe investment like a savings account or money market. When your current car's maintenance bills are greater than your monthly payment, then it's time for a newer car. Use the money in your car fund as a down payment.

Once your credit cards are all paid off, you can use that extra money to pay off the car loan more quickly or to build up your car fund again. Each time you go through the process you'll have more money in the fund when it's time to buy a new car. Eventually you'll be able to pay cash. A really neat thing.

You can also apply this principle to any other loans you have. Just keep in mind that your goal is to be debt free.

STEP 3. FIND THE RIGHT HOME

Many individuals spend too much on their homes. It's better to rent than to live in constant worry about how to keep up with a home mortgage *and* put food on the table. Renting has some other benefits, and makes sense in some circumstances. For example, if you need flexibility to move within the next few years—whether due to job transfers, family issues, or whatever—then renting may be the right choice. It can be tough to sell a home in a hurry if you need to, and you'll incur transaction costs when you sell your home as well as when you buy a new one.

With that said, I prefer home ownership. When you think long term, it becomes clear that when you are debt free and own your home you can withstand a lot of financial turmoil. Unemployment, stock market upheaval, soaring gas prices, or whatever, unexpected hits on your budget are easier to take when you don't have a monthly housing payment.

So how much should you spend on your home? The expense guidelines in Chapter 5, "Your Spending Plan," will give you some common recommendations for the maximum amount to allocate for a monthly payment. Keep in mind, those recommendations are for the *maximum* amount. If you spend less, you will have more dollars to put toward investing in your financial future in other ways that can provide a return on investment and that may also reduce your taxes, which will make still more money available for you to work with. A house can be a great long-term investment—*if* you buy in the right place, at the right time, and the housing market moves in your favor. But more often than not, it's not the best investment purely from a financial perspective. That's why it makes sense to buy as much house as you need, but not more than you need.

Even so, there is a lot to be said for having a place you can call your own that's paid for. I think you should strive for that.

Step 4: Prepare for a Rainy Day

You can make all the best choices about handling your money—you spend less than you make, you manage your debt wisely, and you've found a home that makes sense—but let's face it, stuff happens. You could lose your job. You might become disabled. You may even die early. (Some say it's always early.) No one's life is so charmed that it proceeds happily along without an unforeseen detour at some point...or several.

Since you know you're likely to encounter your share of obstacles or setbacks along the way, it only makes sense to prepare yourself ahead of time. If you were going on a backpacking trip, knowing there was a chance of rain while you're up on the mountain, you'd pack your rain gear and some dry clothes, right? When it's your financial future we're talking about, a special account called a "cash reserve" is your equivalent of rain gear and dry clothes. Think of it as a way to protect yourself as you travel life's path of changeable weather. Let me explain how simple this step is—and why it's so important.

One of the surest ways to throw you off your path to becoming More than a Millionaire is to lose your income for an extended period of time. Heck...never mind your long-term retirement plans, losing your job could have severe consequences in the near term, such as getting you thrown out of your home. But the reality is that things like that happen. Even if you have a job you love, and you expect to keep it until they buy you that retirement watch, you could face an illness or injury that makes it impossible for you to work. Or the business you work for might have to downsize, and you could be out of work in a tough job market. Suddenly you're not just struggling to save for retirement—you're trying to figure out how to pay the mortgage.

You need a way to get through an extended but temporary loss of income—a tent for a rainy day until the squall subsides. The equity in your house doesn't serve your purpose here, because you can't turn that into spendable cash without selling your house or going into debt. And you certainly don't want to be forced to live on credit cards while you get back on your feet. But if you prepare ahead of time by setting aside money for the sole purpose of seeing you through that sort of a rainy day, you'll be able to get through it relatively unscathed.

It's easy enough to do. Just set aside a portion of every paycheck in a special account designated as your cash reserve account, specifically for this purpose, until you have enough to get you through that rainy day. How much is enough? It varies somewhat, depending on your unique circumstances. But a good rule of thumb is to reserve an amount equivalent to three to six months of your monthly expenses. A word of caution here—don't guess how much your monthly expenses are. This is not the time to set yourself up for an unpleasant surprise. Take an accurate reading of how much you *actually* spend each month. In Chapter 5, "Your Spending Plan," we'll look at a way to identify your monthly expenses, and you can use that number as a starting point.

Once you know what all your monthly expenses are, total those up and multiply that amount by 3, then multiply the total monthly expenses again by 6. The results of those two calculations will give you a range to aim for in your cash reserve account. If you have a two-income family, and you and your partner work at different places, you're probably safe to use the lesser amount that reflects three months of expenses, because it's unlikely both of you will lose your income at the same time. If you have a one-income family, or a two-income family with both of you working at the same place— which means both of you could lose your income at the same time— then it's a good idea to maintain your reserves closer to the high end of that range.

Once you begin to establish your cash reserve, put it into an account you can access quickly. We've already established that the equity in your house won't do it for you. But there are other options. A designated checking account (separate from the one you use for routine expenses), a savings account, a money market, short-term CDs (with terms less than 12 months), or Treasury Bills will do the trick. (See more about these types of investments in the "Cash Investments" section, beginning on page 90 in Chapter 6, "The Basic Types of Investments.")

STEP 5: CREATE A SHELTER AGAINST FINANCIAL STORMS

There are things in your life that you just can't afford to lose. Your income is one of those, and your cash reserve fund is a way to protect yourself from the impact of a loss of income. But if you lose your home, your car, your health...or even your life...the financial setback to you and your family could be insurmountable.

Fortunately there's a way to create a shelter against the risk of losses like those. It's called "risk management" or, to most of us, insurance. It allows you to divert those catastrophic losses to someone else—an insurance company. Of course, the company will charge you a fee for assuming that risk on your behalf, and that fee is your insurance premium. Yes, I know it can be painful to spend a chunk of your hard-earned cash on insurance premiums. But as someone who has lost his home and everything in it to an F5 tornado...I can promise you it's important.

It's easy enough to assume it'll never happen to you. I admit there was a time when I felt that way, too. But you can't imagine what it's like to lose every material possession—until you do. The emotional toll that comes with an experience like that is tough. But if an insurance company is there to help you recoup your financial loss, I guarantee you'll recognize that those premiums were some of the best money you've ever spent.

You don't even need to take a catastrophic hit like an F5 tornado to benefit from a good insurance policy. If you've never been in a fender bender, you'll be stunned to learn what it costs to repair a corner panel on your car. (Yes, I just found out.) It's enough to throw you off track for quite a long time.

So it's just smart planning to secure your financial future by putting some money toward a few basic insurance policies. It's also important to choose your coverage wisely. As any enthusiastic insurance salesperson will tell you, there are more types of insurance than there are spots on a leopard (well, almost...), and each one comes with a range of options for *how much* coverage you can buy. You could easily spend your whole paycheck on premiums. We can't possibly cover all your options in this book—after all, it's a book about becoming More than a Millionaire, not about the world of insurance. (Others have written bigger books than this one on just that subject alone.) What I can do for you here is point you toward the basic types of insurance you're most likely to need. You can then take that list and find the coverage that's best suited to your unique circumstances and needs.

Here are the types of insurance you should consider:

- Life insurance
- Long-term disability insurance
- Homeowners insurance (or renters insurance)
- Auto insurance
- Health insurance
- Umbrella protection

Let me share a few thoughts on each.

Life insurance.

When you die, your family will lose your income, as well as the many other benefits—financial and otherwise—of having you around. If you're married, and your spouse dies first, you'll be left to manage the loss—financial and otherwise. When you buy life insurance, you transfer the financial risks associated with that death to the insurance company. When you or your significant other passes on, the insurer will pay the beneficiary an amount of money you agree on when you buy the policy.

There are two basic kinds of life insurance: whole life and term life.[13] When you buy a whole life insurance policy, it's with the expectation you'll keep it for your lifetime, and your premiums remain the same for the life of the policy. Whole life policies accumulate cash value you can borrow against, or you can cash in the policy for a small portion of the money you've paid in. A term life policy guarantees your premium will remain the same for a set period of time, or term; when the term is over, you can usually renew the policy, but your premiums are likely to increase—quite possibly to an unaffordable amount. A term policy accumulates no cash value, so the insurance company only pays if you die during the term of the policy.

At first glance, it may seem that the whole life policy is a much better deal. But because there's a high likelihood the company will eventually have to pay that death benefit, premiums are much higher than a term policy with the same benefit amount—sometimes ten or even twenty times higher. And while the cash value that comes with many whole life policies may seem attractive, in my opinion there are far better ways for you to invest your money to accumulate cash.

I prefer term life insurance, for a few reasons. Term life coverage is pure and simple protection for what you need at this stage of your life. Because premiums are so much cheaper, you can get more protection for your premium dollars than you can with a whole life policy. And since you have flexibility in the length of the

---

[13] There's also universal life, variable life, single premium, mortgage protection, and more, but whole life and term life are all you need to be concerned about for now.

term, you can choose a policy that will cover you for the risks you're most concerned about for the time frame you need. For example, if you have young children you can get a twenty-year term policy. That means your premium will remain the same for twenty years. At the end of that time the premium will increase substantially—but by that time your kids will be grown and on their own, and if you've stuck with your savings plan you will have accumulated investments so your need for life insurance will be significantly reduced or even eliminated.

Long-term disability insurance.
We've talked about how important it is to have a cash reserve equivalent to three to six months of your income. That will get you through if you're sick or injured and can't work for a few months. But what if a more serious illness or injury keeps you out of work for more than six months...maybe a year or even longer?

That's where long-term disability insurance will protect you. It's extremely important, and the majority of people overlook it. A long-term disability policy will pay a portion of your lost income if your disability lasts beyond a certain waiting period. The percentage of income it pays and the waiting period vary—as you might expect, premiums go up as the amount of benefit payment goes up and the waiting period goes down.

So...what terms are best? Even if you wanted to pay for full replacement of your income, that's not an option. Insurers pay only a percentage of your lost income as an incentive for you to go back to work, if you can. And since you have your cash reserve on hand to cover you for a few months, you have the option to save on premiums by, in effect, self-insuring for those first few months. The general rule, then, is to insure 66% of your income with a 6-month waiting period.

There's one other important consideration for any policy you buy: Be sure to look at the definition of disability. Does it sound reasonable? If it says you have to be deaf, dumb, blind, and quadriplegic before they pay you a dime, then the premium may be enticingly low, but it's not a good policy. Look for something that would protect you if you're genuinely unable to do your job.

Homeowners and renters insurance.

I've already told you I lost my home and everything in it to an F5 tornado, so you can guess where I come down on this. Homeowners insurance is critical, and if you have a mortgage your lender will require it. If your house is damaged or, heaven forbid, completely lost, this coverage will pay you money to repair or rebuild it, and also for the loss of your personal property. If you rent your home, renters insurance is just as essential. Like homeowners insurance, it covers loss of the contents of your home—that's right, all of the personal belongings you keep inside your house or apartment. (Either coverage may even protect you if an item is lost or stolen outside your home, such as from your car.)

Some policies pay the replacement value of the structure or its contents, others pay only the actual cash value. That's a big difference. While a market-value policy is likely to be cheaper than one that pays replacement value, you may end up without enough cash to make your home habitable again. And a check for the actual cash value of your wardrobe and other personal items won't go very far when it's time to shop for replacements. That's why I like policies that pay replacement value.

Don't be tempted to save a few dollars by opting for a smaller amount of coverage for your contents. I had the maximum allowable, and it still wasn't enough. Your situation may be different, but do your best beforehand to make sure your policy is adequate. Take the time to go through your house and calculate how much it really would cost you to replace everything you use. It's probably quite a bit more than you expect. It's also a good idea to make an inventory of the more expensive items, and take a photograph or video of the inside of your home and your closets. Those records will make it easier to prove your losses should you ever have to make a claim.

One thing you can safely do to keep your premiums lower is to choose a large deductible. For a homeowners or renters policy I'd go with at least $1,000. Think about it—an insurance company incurs the greatest financial liability with the first dollars of risk it assumes, because you're more likely to have a $500 loss than a $20,000 loss. So it follows that they charge you far more for those first few hundred dollars of coverage. Some people call this "trading dollars" with the insurance company—you pay a nice fat premium and they almost always pay you something back, because it doesn't take much of a loss to trigger a claim. But when you trade dollars with the insurance company, who do you think comes out ahead? (Hint: It isn't you.)

A better strategy is to choose a higher deductible and assume that initial, inexpensive, small risk yourself. You'll save a nice amount of cash that you can use toward your other financial goals. You can also think of your cash reserve fund as a sort of self-insurance fund, and tap into that to cover your deductible if you need to.

Your homeowners or renters insurance policy also has liability coverage for you and your family. This protects against stuff like slip-and-fall injuries, that golf ball your son put through the neighbor's bay window...things like that.

Auto insurance.

A thorough discussion of the many aspects of car insurance could fill an entire book in and of itself. Fortunately you don't need to know all the fine points to make sound decisions about what kind of auto policy to buy and how much coverage you need.

A basic auto insurance policy usually includes three main types of protection:

- Comprehensive and collision coverage (fondly known as "comp and collision") protects you in the event of damage to or loss of the vehicle itself, whether it's the result of a car accident, a theft, a tree falling on your car, or...yes, an F5 tornado. Your comp and collision coverage will protect you regardless of who is at fault.

- Liability coverage will pay for injury to another person or damage to someone else's property, if the injury or damage occurs as a result of an accident you caused. This is without a doubt the part of your auto insurance policy that's most crucial to your long-term financial well-being. If you're responsible for an accident in which someone is injured, you could literally be ruined forever. Most states require every driver to carry liability coverage but, whether your state does or not, if you drive a car you simply must buy it. Period.

- Medical coverage pays for medical expenses or funeral costs for the driver or passengers in the car.

You can also buy a host of other types of coverage, including payments for a rental car for you to drive while yours is getting that fender replaced, roadside assistance, uninsured motorist coverage in case someone without insurance rear-ends you at a stop light, and lots more. Take time to review the cost and benefits of each of those to decide what's right for you.

As with homeowners and renters insurance, the best way to keep your premiums at a manageable level is to choose high deductibles.

Health insurance.

Health insurance is another topic that could fill a book, and it's constantly changing. Once again, the high deductible is preferable. How high? Of course it depends on your situation. One way to approach it is to look at how long your employer will continue to pay your salary (presumably as "sick days") if you're unable to work, and calculate how much money that will be—that's money you won't have to take from your cash reserve account for living expenses, so you can use it to pay your deductible instead. If you don't have paid sick leave, or don't have enough, you might consider increasing your cash reserve by an amount equivalent to your deductible. One way or another, you can't afford the cost of major surgery or a long hospital stay, so you simply must find a health insurance policy you can afford. Choosing one with a high deductible is a way to do that. Just be sure you have a plan in place for how you'll pay that deductible if you need to.

Because the world of health insurance is constantly and rapidly changing, I suggest you visit www.Health.com and www.healthcare.gov to learn the latest details.

Umbrella liability insurance.

An umbrella liability policy can be issued as a rider on your homeowners or renters policy, and it provides additional coverage over and above the basic liability coverage in those, as well as in your auto policy. It pays only after the underlying policy limits are used up, so it's relatively inexpensive for the coverage limits it offers. It also provides protection for some types of claims not covered by the underlying policy.

For example, suppose your wonderful, sweet, gentle dog goes exploring and wanders into the neighbor's yard. Your neighbor, who is somewhat less sweet and gentle, grabs the dog by the collar and starts yanking the poor yelping pup off his feet. Your frightened little pal tries to escape, and bites the neighbor in the process—so of course said neighbor sues you, and you must get a lawyer to defend yourself.

If this incident had happened on your property, your basic homeowners policy would probably cover it. But since your dog was in the neighbor's yard, that's unlikely. This is where an umbrella policy would kick in. Since anything related to liability can quickly become ruinously expensive, an umbrella policy is a must. I suggest a limit of $500,000 or more.

Finding an Agent

It's essential that you find an insurance agent you can trust, who will become part of your professional financial team. The key is finding someone with integrity, someone you can count on to be there when you need him...someone who will go to bat for you.

I found out just how valuable an agent is when I filed a claim after the tornado. He went to bat for my family in a lot of areas that I couldn't handle myself, or didn't know I *could* handle myself. For example, immediately after the tornado my agent delivered a basic check to us and told us about "loss of use"—the part of our coverage that paid for a place for my family to live when we'd lost the use of our house. Our agent put us at ease, using the resources at his disposal to let us know we would be okay. He was there to look at the damage to our home (or what was left of it) and helped us change adjusters when the first one was, shall we say, performing less than optimally.

All of this is only to say how important it is to choose your insurance agent—and all your advisors—wisely. If you don't already know one you feel certain you can trust, start searching for one. I prefer independent agents...slightly. These are usually self-employed people who own or work in an agency that represents several different insurance companies, as opposed to an agent who is an employee of a single insurance company. They can shop your needs among many different companies, and they're not as likely to be swayed by pressure from any one company. Ask around, get referrals, sit down and meet with a few or several. Once you find someone you like and trust, stick with him or her.

First Things First

These first five steps toward becoming More than a Millionaire are exactly where you need to start on your path toward securing your financial future—and you can begin taking them today.

First, make the choice, right here and now, to stop spending more than you make. Put those credit cards on ice (go ahead, do it now...I'll wait), then go online and review all your credit accounts, make a list of the outstanding balance on each one, and decide which one you'll pay down first.

Then, take stock of your housing situation. If you don't already own a home, decide if now is the time to take the leap. Whether you rent or own, use the expense guidelines in the spending plan in Chapter 5 to make sure your housing costs aren't preventing you from reaching your financial goals.

Next, it's time to begin allocating money toward your cash reserve account and insurance premiums, so you're ready for a rainy day as well as a catastrophic financial storm. But what will you do first? Should you put your money toward six months of income in your cash reserve, or buy a life insurance policy to provide your spouse—or you—with income when one of you dies? Or is it more important to beef up the liability coverage on your auto and homeowners policies?

Once again, every aspect of financial planning is personal, and those choices are best made by you and a financial advisor who knows your unique circumstances and has your best interest at heart. What I can do for you here is offer some guidelines that make sense for most people under most scenarios.

First and foremost, you need insurance to protect your health, your auto, and your home. That's not optional unless you don't have them—and while you may not have a car, even renters need renters insurance. And health insurance just isn't up for discussion.

After that, though, the choices get more complicated. Have a family? Then life insurance is a must. If you don't, then I would say work on your cash reserve, buy disability coverage and an umbrella policy, in that order. Beyond that, it really comes down to assessing your needs, where your greatest risks of loss lie, and what you can fit into your budget.

How Will You Make It All Happen? A Spending Plan

You can't manage your money effectively if you don't know how you spend it, or if you don't make conscious decisions about how you want to spend it. There are too many choices out there, and too many temptations that can lead you to spend money today on things you don't need, instead of investing it in your future. Operating without a plan and buying on impulse are among the biggest reasons so many people never become financially secure, even when they make a steady income.

But it doesn't have to be that way. You can step out of that trap by taking control of your spending habits, to put your money where it will benefit you the most and help you realize your goals.

- First, you need to identify where your money goes, and get a handle on what your spending habits are.
- Second, you'll want to set short-term goals for the best way to allocate your funds, so that you make sure you put money first and foremost toward the things that will help you realize your long-term goal of becoming More than a Millionaire.

There are some great strategies for developing a workable spending plan that's easy to use and effective. I'll give you all the details on how to do it in Chapter 5. For now, just know that having a plan and sticking to it will make it easy for you to take those essential first steps on your path to success.

CHAPTER 5

YOUR SPENDING PLAN

Ultimately, taking control of your financial future is all about making smart choices about how you manage your money today. Chances are you know exactly how much you bring in every month. You might even have a pretty good idea how much you spend each month. (Let me guess...those two numbers are about the same, right?) But if you're like most people, you'd be hard pressed to say *where* that money goes—and there's precious little going into a retirement fund that will eventually allow you to reach your goal of becoming More than a Millionaire. You probably even believe there just isn't enough left over after you pay your "necessary" expenses to be able to set aside any serious money for your future.

I'm here to challenge you on that last one. Without knowing how much money you make, how much you spend, or what you spend it on, I'm willing to bet you *do* have enough to start saving for your retirement. It's all about making smart choices—the operative word here being "choices."

Every single day you make choices about how you spend your money. For most people, each choice is driven by a desire to acquire something, here and now, in this moment. They decide what they want, then figure out how to pay for it. Whether it's the latté on the way to work, the ready-to-eat dinners for nights when there's no time to cook, or a smart new suit to wear to that meeting with the boss, they spend money on things that feel important today. But when today's wants and needs (at least they seem like "needs") drive those choices, long-term goals like retirement never quite make it into the equation. So that latté in effect takes priority over your ability to retire comfortably. Is that really what you want?

You can take control of your financial future simply by switching around the way you decide what to buy today. Instead of deciding what you want and then finding a way to pay for it, what if you first decide how much money you have available to spend, and then buy only what you can afford? That way you'll know for sure you're putting enough money toward the things that matter most, such as securing your financial future. If becoming More than a Millionaire is really a priority for you, you can in fact make it happen. All you need to do is plan for it, and let that be reflected in your daily spending choices—set aside the money for what really matters, then spend what's left on the things that are nice but not necessary.

What Do You Spend Your Money On?

The first step in taking control of your spending is finding out what your spending habits are. Where does your money go? If you don't keep track of it, then you don't know. The second step is to create a careful plan that will tell you how much you can afford to spend on what, and still remain on track to reach your goals to become More than a Millionaire.

You can do both by setting up a spending plan. It's a tool for tracking the money you actually spend every day, and also for making clear choices about how much you want to spend on what. Some people call it a budget, but that makes it sound more like self-imposed drudgery than the key to financial freedom that it is. I'm not overselling it here: Your spending plan is the key to having the future you want.

There are plenty of ways to set up a spending plan, and I'll talk you through the mechanics of it as we go along. But however you set it up, it's my experience as a financial advisor that, for a plan to be effective, it needs to be simple to understand and easy to use on an ongoing basis. The spending plan I'm going to share with you is super simple and only takes about two hours a month to maintain.

To get you started, let's explore the various ways we all spend money. To make your plan easy to work with, I've divided all your spending into three main categories. Then we'll break each of those down into subcategories. Let's begin with the big chunks:

- First Things First: Charitable Giving and Paying Yourself
- Fixed and Ongoing Expenses
- Living Expenses

Now let's look at the various types of expenses within each main category.

First Things First:
Charitable Giving and Paying Yourself First

Charitable giving. It may sound odd to start a spending plan by giving money away, but I do. It's up to you, of course, to decide whether or not to include it, but I highly encourage you to do so. I honestly believe that no matter what your income is, you can give back...share your good fortune to support a worthy cause. The rule of thumb is to donate at least 10% of your income. My experience has been that when I have done so with the right attitude, giving with a cheerful heart and an awareness of my abundance—and without giving just to reap some reward in return—it comes back many times over. It's happened to me time and time again, and as an advisor I've seen the same thing happen to others. There is no logical explanation for it. It's just the way things work.

If you're not in the habit of giving money to charity, you might not feel very cheerful about giving away cash just for the sake of giving it away...and frankly, I wouldn't want you to do that. I do want you to give your money to a charity that means something to you, to a cause you genuinely care about. I'm certain there's an issue you've thought about a lot, or that tugs at your heart strings—and I'm equally certain there's an organization doing some meaningful work in that arena. Maybe you're concerned about the plight of homeless people in your community, or the difficulties foster kids face...or maybe you want to support bringing clean water to a struggling village in Africa, or help fund a local shelter and adoption center for companion animals. No matter what cause you're interested in, there's likely a related effort underway that would benefit greatly from a few extra dollars every month. Contributing a few of your own hard-earned dollars to support that effort will benefit it and you in ways you probably can't foresee.

Paying yourself first. I don't have to tell you there are countless places to put your money from one paycheck to the next. Every day, someone or something wants to claim a few—or a lot—of your dollars. Too often there are more demands on your money than there are dollars to go around. In that scenario, the only way to make sure some of that money goes toward securing your financial well-being is to pay yourself first. That's right. Before you spend your hard-earned cash on entertainment, to buy groceries, or even to pay your mortgage or rent and other bills, set something aside to make sure you have cash on hand for emergencies now, and for your retirement at some point down the road.

- **Savings.** This is money you allocate each month to create your cash reserve. As we discussed in Chapter 4, under "Prepare for a rainy day" on page 45, a cash reserve is money you set aside for emergency purposes, and you should build it up to an amount equal to three to six months of your monthly expenses. Once your cash reserve fund reaches that amount, then you can redirect that monthly allocation toward debt reduction or into retirement plans that save taxes. Remember to put your cash reserve money into something that's liquid, like a savings account or short-term CD, so you can access the money quickly if you need to.

- **Investments.** This is money you set aside each month to go into a long-term investment account. It's literally your retirement fund, so you can see why it's an essential part of your More than a Millionaire strategy. Generally it is best to place these dollars in a retirement account that saves you money on taxes.

Fixed and Ongoing Expenses

There are three types of fixed and ongoing payments you make once each month.

- **Housing.** Housing is a monthly expense that includes your mortgage payment or rent, utilities (water, gas, electric, and phone), and property taxes if you own your home. (If your homeowners insurance is included with your mortgage payment, you'll need to subtract it out and add it back in under the insurance category.)

- **Debt Payments.** These are payments other than your mortgage. This could include credit card payments, car payments, student loans, and so forth. We took a close look at the importance of getting out of debt in Chapter 4, under "Manage Debt Wisely" on page 39, and this part of your spending plan is designed to do that for you. If you doubt that this is important, please go back and read that section in Chapter 4 again. Once you've paid off your debts, money allocated here can go into your investment account.

- **Insurance.** This expense can be tough to control, often because we're sold insurance instead of buying what we really need. For your spending plan, this category will include your homeowners or renters insurance, and your umbrella, life, health, and disability insurance. (If you're not sure which of these you need, refer back to Chapter 4, "Create a Shelter Against Financial Storms" on page 47.) Don't include your car insurance here—that belongs in the "Transportation" category, below.

Living Expenses

Of course, there are many other ways you spend your money besides charitable giving, housing, debt, and insurance. Some of those happen monthly, but many happen more or less often. For expenses that arise less than once a month, or even just once or twice a year, calculate the amount you'll spend annually then divide it by twelve, and use that amount as your monthly allocation. Whenever they occur, you'll need to track them, too, as you work to monitor where your money is going. Here are some examples of the types of expenses you'll track. (NOTE: Some items could really fall into two or more categories. Choose the category that makes the most sense to you, and keep it there. What's most important is that you are consistent with where you place the expense, and that you understand how you budgeted for it.)

- **Food.** This is your grocery bill. It also includes those meals you eat away from home because you're hungry—not for recreation. If you buy a sandwich for lunch in the middle of your workday, that expense would go here.

- **Transportation.** This includes your car or motorcycle payment, insurance, gas, and maintenance. In a perfect world, it would also include a small fund to replace your current vehicle or get a better one. The goal is to eventually pay cash for your vehicle and not have a loan. (See my suggestion for how to make that happen on page 43 in Chapter 4.)

- **Entertainment and Recreation.** This category includes dining out for entertainment, such as a night out with family or friends. It also includes money you spend on vacations, hobbies, sporting events, movies, camping, and so forth.

- **Clothing.** Since you don't really buy clothes every month (you don't, do you?), take your annual expenditure and divide it by twelve, then enter that amount for your monthly allotment. Be careful not to buy all your clothes at the beginning of the year, as it will leave you short of cash in the early months—and potentially short of a winter coat in November.

- **Medical.** This is for any out-of-pocket costs for medical care—not your health insurance premium. (That's in your "Fixed and Ongoing Expenses," on page 67.) It might include over-the-counter drugs, deductibles you need to pay before your insurance kicks in, or health related items not covered by insurance, such as an orthodontist's care or eyeglasses. These expenses usually arise in chunks, at random times throughout the year rather than monthly, which is why it's important to set money aside for them each month so you won't be hit with a big bill you can't pay.

- **School Tuition and Child Care.** Tuition may be for school for yourself or your spouse, or your children's private school. This allotment is also for your day care or a sitter. If you do not have expenses here, redirect the budgeted amount to the other expense items.

- **Miscellaneous.** This is a catch-all area you can use when an expense doesn't seem to fit anywhere else. Examples could be gifts, a trip to the beauty salon, massages...that sort of thing.

EXPENSE GUIDELINES FOR YOUR INCOME LEVEL —NOW AND AS YOUR INCOME GROWS

Knowing exactly how you spend your money is the essential first step in gaining control of your spending habits and making wise choices about how you allocate your available funds. But how will you know if you're making wise choices or not? How much is too much to spend on entertainment or clothes...or housing, for that matter?

The following tables provide some guidelines for a reasonable amount to spend in each of the categories we discussed above, depending on your income. The amounts are listed as a percentage of your net monthly income—that is, your take-home pay after taxes. So if you make $30,000 but after taxes you have $27,000, then your 10% allocation for charitable giving would be $2,700 (because

27,000 x 0.10 = 2,700). The guidelines suggest 5% of your net income for insurance, so you would allocate $1,350 (because 27,000 x 0.05 = 1,350). If you find you're spending much more than the recommended amount in any area, you'll want to evaluate that area to see if you can bring your expenses closer to the guidelines.

Each table covers a specific income bracket, and all the tables include guidelines for three types of households: a single person, a family of two adults without children, or a family of four. Please keep in mind that the listed percentages are *only* guidelines. Use them to help you find areas where you may be spending more than you should, to identify where you're doing well, or just to give yourself a target to aim for.

An Easy Guide to Percentages

If you're not an accountant, an engineer, or a mortgage lender, you may be like a lot of people whose eyes glaze over at the thought of calculating a percentage of anything. If you get a knot in your stomach when you try to figure out what it means to budget 26% of your income for housing, rest easy. It's much, much easier than you think.

You own a calculator, right? (If not, please go buy one—or at least download an app for your phone.) Then all you need to do is convert the percentage number into a calculator-friendly format. It's really simple. Just take the percentage number, like 26%, drop the "%" sign, and divide it by 100 on your calculator. For our example, 26 divided by 100 is 0.26.

$$26 \div 100 = 0.26$$

An Easy Guide to Percentages, continued:

Your percentage number is now in a calculator-friendly, decimal format. Just multiply 0.26 by your net income to find out how much you can spend on housing.

Let's say your gross income is $30,000, and your net income is $27,000. Your calculation would look like this:

$$0.26 \times 27,000 = 7,020$$

So 26% of $27,000 is $7,020. You can spend $7,020 a year on a mortgage or rent. Divide $7,020 by 12 (because there are 12 months in a year) and you find you can spend $585 each month on housing.

See how easy?

Let's try another example. We'll assume again that your take-home pay is $27,000, and you're single. I recommend you allocate 6% of your income toward entertainment and recreation. To figure out how much money that is, drop the "%" sign from 6%, and use your calculator to divide 6 by 100, which gives you 0.06.

$$6 \div 100 = 0.06$$

Then multiply 0.06 by your income, like this:

$$0.06 \times 27,000 = 1,620$$

So your annual entertainment budget is $1,620. Divide that number by 52 (because there are 52 weeks in a year), and you'll see you have $31.15 each week to spend on going out to dinner with friends or to allocate for your annual vacation.

IF YOUR GROSS INCOME IS $25,000 - $35,000			
AND YOU ARE:	SINGLE ADULT	TWO ADULTS	FAMILY OF FOUR
ALLOCATE THIS % OF YOUR NET INCOME:			
First Things First:			
Charitable Giving	10%	10%	10%
Savings	5%	5%	4%
Investments	4%	2%	1%
Fixed & Ongoing Expenses:			
Housing	26%	28%	30%
Debt Payments	6%	5%	4%
Insurance	5%	5%	5%
Living Expenses:			
Food	12%	13%	12%
Transportation	12%	13%	13%
Ent./Recreation	6%	5%	3%
Clothing	4%	4%	2%
Medical	4%	4%	4%
School/Child Care[14]	4%	4%	10%
Miscellaneous	2%	2%	2%
Total %	100%	100%	100%

[14] If you have child care expenses, you may qualify for a Child Care Credit on your taxes. When you fill out your tax return, be sure to look into this and any other available tax credits.

IF YOUR **GROSS** INCOME IS **$35,000 - $55,000**			
AND YOU ARE:	**SINGLE ADULT**	**TWO ADULTS**	**FAMILY OF FOUR**
ALLOCATE THIS % OF YOUR NET INCOME:			
First Things First:			
Charitable Giving	10%	10%	10%
Savings	4%	4%	4%
Investments	7%	6%	5%
Fixed & Ongoing Expenses:			
Housing	23%	24%	27%
Debt Payments	6%	5%	4%
Insurance	5%	5%	5%
Living Expenses:			
Food	10%	12%	13%
Transportation	11%	12%	12%
Ent./Recreation	9%	7%	4%
Clothing	4%	4%	3%
Medical	4%	4%	4%
School/Child Care[15]	4%	4%	7%
Miscellaneous	3%	3%	2%
Total %	100%	100%	100%

---

[15] If you have child care expenses, you may qualify for a Child Care Credit on your taxes. When you fill out your tax return, be sure to look into this and any other available tax credits.

IF YOUR **GROSS** INCOME IS **$55,000 - $75,000**			
AND YOU ARE:	**SINGLE ADULT**	**TWO ADULTS**	**FAMILY OF FOUR**
ALLOCATE THIS % OF YOUR NET INCOME:			
First Things First:			
Charitable Giving	10%	10%	10%
Savings	4%	4%	4%
Investments	12%	10%	9%
Fixed & Ongoing Expenses:			
Housing	20%	21%	23%
Debt Payments	6%	5%	4%
Insurance	5%	5%	5%
Living Expenses:			
Food	9%	11%	11%
Transportation	9%	10%	10%
Ent./Recreation	9%	8%	6%
Clothing	5%	5%	5%
Medical	4%	4%	4%
School/Child Care[16]	4%	4%	5%
Miscellaneous	3%	3%	4%
Total %	100%	100%	100%

---

[16] If you have child care expenses, you may qualify for a Child Care Credit on your taxes. When you fill out your tax return, be sure to look into this and any other available tax credits.

IF YOUR GROSS INCOME IS $75,000 - $95,000			
AND YOU ARE:	**SINGLE ADULT**	**TWO ADULTS**	**FAMILY OF FOUR**
ALLOCATE THIS % OF YOUR NET INCOME:			
First Things First:			
Charitable Giving	10%	10%	10%
Savings	4%	4%	4%
Investments	12%	10%	10%
Fixed & Ongoing Expenses:			
Housing	20%	20%	20%
Debt Payments	7%	6%	6%
Insurance	5%	5%	5%
Living Expenses:			
Food	8%	10%	12%
Transportation	9%	10%	10%
Ent. /Recreation	9%	9%	7%
Clothing	5%	5%	5%
Medical	4%	4%	4%
School/Child Care[17]	4%	4%	4%
Miscellaneous	3%	3%	3%
Total %	100%	100%	100%

Have you run the numbers to see how much you should be spending in some of these categories? If so...I know what you're

---

[17] If you have child care expenses, you may qualify for a Child Care Credit on your taxes. When you fill out your tax return, be sure to look into this and any other available tax credits.

thinking. Yes, it is going to be challenging to stay within these guidelines in some categories. I haven't said it was going to be easy. I am saying, though, that it will be worth it.

Your Spending Plan, Step by Step

Now that you know how to sort your expenses into categories, and about how much you should be spending in each one, how will you actually make it all work for you? Remember, we said that a good spending plan involves discovering how much you actually spend, then making smart choices about how much you *want* to spend. There are computer programs and apps you can use to help you do both of those. A program called Quicken is a nice one, and if you're into computers that may be the way to go. However, I'd like to show you a very simple paper method first, because if you can understand how it works on paper, it'll be much easier to transition to a computer program if you decide to go that route.

Here's how to set up the paper method, step by step:

1. First, buy a small, lined, pocket notebook. I like the small Moleskine notebooks. If you really use this system, you will more than make up the cost of the notebook in the first week.

2. On page 1, write your name, the year, and the quote, "If you keep score, the score will improve."

3. On page 2, on the left-hand side of the page, list all of the spending categories we discussed earlier in this chapter, along with an abbreviation for each one, as follows:

1. Charitable Giving (CG)

2. Savings (Sv)

3. Investments (Inv)

4. Housing (H)

5. Debt Payments (D)

6. Insurance (Ins)

7. Food (F)

8. Transportation (T)

9. Entertainment/Recreation (E)

10. Clothing (Cl)

11. Medical (M)

12. School/Child Care (SCC)

13. Miscellaneous (Misc)

4. Now, consider your situation, and decide what time frame you'd like to use to plan your spending. That is, do you want to track your expenses weekly, bi-weekly, monthly, semi-monthly, or something else? Most people use a time frame that's the same as their pay period, so they can allocate expenses out of each paycheck. But use whatever is convenient for you.

   At the top of page 2, above your list of all the spending categories, write your preferred time frame—weekly, monthly, or whatever.

5. Next, look at the spending plan expense guideline for your income level, and use those percentages to calculate how much money you should spend in each spending category for your chosen time frame. Enter those numbers on the right side of page 2, opposite the appropriate category. You're looking for the

actual dollar amount here, so apply the guideline percentages to your net (after-tax) income.

Let's stick with our assumption that your gross annual salary is $30,000, and your after-tax income is $27,000. Let's say you get paid twice a month, or 24 times a year, and your take-home pay on each paycheck is $1,125 (because 27,000 ÷ 24 = 1,125). The guidelines suggest you allocate 10% of your net income to charitable giving, so on the right side of page 2, across from the "Charitable Giving"

My Spending Plan Expense allocations for each pay period (semi-monthly)		
1. Charitable Giving (CG)	10%	$112.50
2. Savings (Sv)	5%	$56.25
3. Investments (Inv)	4%	$45.00
4. Housing (H)	26%	$292.50
5. Debt Payments (D)	6%	$67.50
6. Insurance (Ins)	5%	$56.25
7. Food (F)	12%	$135.00
8. Transportation (T)	12%	$135.00
9. Entertainment/Recreation (E)	6%	$67.50
10. Clothing (Cl)	4%	$45.00
11. Medical (M)	4%	$45.00
12. School/Child Care (SCC)	4%	$45.00
13. Miscellaneous (Misc)	2%	$22.50

Sample page 2 of your Spending Plan based on:
$30,000 gross annual salary, $27,000 net annual income,
$1125.00 net income per each semi-monthly pay period

category, enter $112.50. Apply the same process to each spending category.

6. Turn to page 3 in your notebook. This is where you'll begin logging how much you actually spend. Across the top of the page, write the actual dates of the first time frame in which you'll keep track of your expenses. Use the same amount of time you chose in step 4—weekly, bi-weekly, monthly, or whatever works for you. If you decided on a monthly time frame, label this page with the current month and year. If you chose bi-weekly, semi-monthly, or something else, label it with dates that correspond to that time frame. If you chose a time frame based on how often you get paid, write down the actual dates of your next pay period.

7. Now take the pocket notebook with you and write down your expenses—all of them—beginning on page 3. Keep a running list for the duration of your chosen time period. For each expense, list the following:

    - the date you spent the money
    - who you paid
    - what it was for
    - the amount you paid
    - and the category of the expense (use those abbreviations you included for each category on page 2)

For example, if you buy a sandwich for lunch on January 2, in your notebook you might write:

1/2 Jimmy John's Café, sandwich $9.75 F

Some expenses don't come along at regular intervals, but rather happen once or twice a year or, like medical expenses, at intervals you can't predict. That's okay, but you still need to plan for them, so you need to count proportionate amounts as expenses during each time frame. If your car insurance comes due in November, you should allocate a proportionate amount of that yearly expense in each spending plan time frame, so when November comes, you're ready.

Let's say your annual car insurance premium is $600 (to make my math easy). If you're paid twice a month, you have 24 pay periods in which to budget for that annual premium. So, every pay period, you will budget $25 (because 600 ÷ 24 = 25). It's far easier to budget $25 every pay period than to come up with $600 when your insurance premium comes due it. Just remember to set that money aside in a separate account, so you don't spend it on something else.

Expenses for January 1 - January 15	
1/1	JC Property Management, rent - $525 H
	Mia Pizzaria, pizza delivery - $16 F
1/2	SpeedyMart, gasoline fill-up - $32.29 T
	Jimmy John's Café, sandwich - $9.75 F
	National Cellular Network, cell phone bill - $41.21 H
	Midwest Gas & Electric, gas and electricity - 44.20 H
	Oklahoma Wireless, internet service - $49.50 H
	ShelterWide Insurance Co., renter's insurance - $23.65 I
	Safe Driver Insurance Co., car insurance - $57.80 T
	Universal Cable Service, cable TV - $72.90 E
1/3	Aroma Roasters, coffee - $3.19 F
1/4	--
1/5	Green Clean, dry cleaning - $6.75 C
	Fresh for You, Chinese take-out - $12.00 F
1/6	Natural Food Co-op, groceries - $56.79 F
	Hometown Hardware, snow shovel - $18.92 H
	Seeds to Trees, vegetable starts, grow light - $23.21 F
	Grab 'n Go, sandwich - $7.05 F
	Bayside Grill, dinner with Sue - $23.00 E
1/7	Child Save Worldwide, donation - $20.00 CG
1/8	SpeedyMart, gasoline fill-up - $18.18 T
1/9	Jimmy John's Café, salad - $8.18 F
	Easy Office Supply, pens, printer paper - $11.26 Misc
	Daily Deal Drug Store, shampoo, nail clippers - $14.65 Misc
1/10	--
1/11	Aroma Roasters, coffee - $3.19 F
	Sue Rogers, game night refreshments - $7.00 E
1/12	Super Taco, burrito take-out - $9.89 F
1/13	Natural Food Co-op, groceries - $63.06 F
	Local Treasures Consignment Shop, sweater - $12.00 C
	The Broccoli Forest, dinner with Jerry - $18.00 E
1/14	--
1/15	SpeedyMart, gasoline fill-up - $20.36 T
	Sample page 3 of your Spending Plan

8. At the end of your first time frame, use a new page to list all your categories again down the left side of the page, and write the total amount you spent on each one in that time frame. It's easy to do—simply go back through all the entries you've made in the past week or two weeks or whatever time frame you chose, identify all the entries you made for a given category, and add them up...then do the same for the next category, and so on.

Compare the totals for each category to the amounts you listed on page 2 of your notebook, based on the expense guidelines.

Total expenses for January 1 – January 15		
	Target amount	How much I spent
1) Charitable Giving (CG)	$112.50	$20.00
2) Savings (Sv)	$56.25	$0
3) Investments (Inv)	$45.00	$0
4) Housing (H)	$292.50	$702.48
5) Debt Payments (D)	$67.50	$0
6) Insurance (Ins)	$56.25	$23.65
7) Food (F)	$135.00	$212.31
8) Transportation (T)	$135.00	$128.63
9) Entertainment/Recreation (E)	$67.50	$120.90
10) Clothing (Cl)	$45.00	$18.75
11) Medical (M)	$45.00	$0
12) School/Child Care (SCC)	$45.00	$0
13) Miscellaneous. (Misc)	$22.50	$25.91
Total:	$1125.00	$1252.63

Are you ahead of your target amounts, or did you overspend a bit? What can you do to improve?

9. Now turn to a fresh page in your notebook, write the dates for your next time frame across the top, and start tracking expenses again. It'll be fun to see if you come closer to your guidelines this time around...and next time, and the time after that.

If this process seems a bit cumbersome at this stage, I promise you it will become an easy part of your routine before long. The thing is, there are so many reasons why it's worth every bit of effort. Just by keeping track, you will spend less. And at the risk of sounding like a broken record, it really and truly is the surest way to make sure you reach your goal of financial freedom. You may find that some people don't get it; friends or co-workers may even kid you about doing this. If so, ask yourself, "Are they going to pay my bills? Are they going to be More than Millionaires?"

How long should you keep track of your spending? Well...I'd suggest you do it until you have so much money you don't need to worry about what you spend. If you make it a habit now to monitor where your money goes, that day will come.

ANALYZING YOUR SPENDING PLAN

Once you have your spending plan in place, and you're making careful choices about how you spend your money and monitoring it as you go, it makes sense to evaluate how you're doing from time to time. There are some financial tools you can use to assess your progress and to help you keep your finances in balance—and also to give you an early indication of any problems. These tools are called "financial ratios," a way of comparing two numbers from your plan to get insight about your progress. Think of these ratios as a financial compass. If you are getting off the path and into danger, the ratios will let you know early enough to give you time to correct the problem and get back on track.

There are hundreds of different financial ratios, but I've whittled them all down to three that are specific to your spending plan. These are the ratios that are most important to you now. They are:

- Saving and investing ratio
- Housing payment ratio
- Total debt payment ratio

In the spending plan guidelines in the early part of this chapter, we used your net income—the amount you take home after taxes—because we were dealing with your actual spendable cash. For these ratios we use your gross income, the amount you're paid *before* taxes, to give us a broader view of your income and expenses. The recommended ratios I've listed here hold true across all income brackets.

Now, let's look at each one....

Saving and investing ratio

This ratio compares how much you save and invest to your gross income. For example, if you save and invest $3,000 a year and make $30,000 a year, your savings rate would be 10%.

$$\$3,000 \div \$30,000 = 0.10 \; or \; 10\%$$

You can also calculate this on a monthly basis if that's easier for you. If you make $2,000 a month and set aside $200 a month for saving and investing, your saving and investing rate is 10%.

$$\$200 \div \$2,000 = 0.10 \; or \; 10\%$$

How much you need to save depends on your goals, your age, how long your income should last...things like that. To reach your goal of financial independence, as a general rule you should aim for saving and investing a minimum of 10% of your income, whether you monitor it on a monthly or annual basis. This, of course, varies depending on your income and situation, but 10% is a great rule of thumb.

Housing payment ratio

This is your housing payment, including taxes and insurance, divided by your gross monthly income. As a general rule, this ratio should never exceed 0.28. Calculating this ratio is a good way to get an idea what your maximum housing payment should be. Just multiply your gross monthly income times 0.28 to get your maximum payment. So if your gross monthly income is $2,000, your housing payment should not exceed $560 a month.

$$\$2000 \; x \; 0.28 = \$560$$

Total debt payment ratio

This is the total of all your monthly debt payments divided by your gross monthly income. Be sure to include *all* your debt payments, like student loans, house payment, car loans, payments on your boat, and so forth. If you have a gross monthly income of $2,000, a house payment of $500, and a car payment of $200 (and no other debt), then your total debt payment ratio would be 0.35.

$$(\$500 + \$200) \div \$2000 = 0.35$$

Your total debt payment ratio should never exceed 0.36.

Where does your money go? Now that you have a spending plan, you'll know. It's up to you to use it, of course, or perhaps use a different plan that works for you. What's the best plan? I'm partial to the one I've laid out in this chapter. But really, the best plan is the one you use. Have a plan and work it. Log your expenses and see where your money goes. That's the one tried and true way to take control of your finances, so you'll stop spending your money on impulse buys you don't care much about. You'll discover you *do* have enough to set aside for the kind of long-term investments that will secure your future today.

Besides, just the simple act of tracking your spending means you'll do better overall. The process, in and of itself, will help you achieve your financial goals of becoming More than a Millionaire.

PART III

TRAVELING DOWN THE PATH

THE VEHICLES YOU WILL USE

 THE BASIC TYPES OF INVESTMENTS

Now that you're reaping the benefits of a solid spending plan, and making smart choices about where your money goes, you've taken the all-important step to allocate money from every paycheck for savings and investments. What will you do with that money? We've talked about putting some into cash investments that you can access on short notice, and some into long-term investments that will become your retirement fund. But those are broad categories, and each has many options to choose from.

It's time to take a closer look at those broad categories to identify the many different options available to you. We'll start by examining three basic types of investments: those cash investments you've heard so much about, and two types of longer-term investments that will make up a majority of your retirement portfolio, as follows:

- Cash investments
- Equity investments, or ownership investments
- Fixed investments, or "loanership" investments

Cash Investments

A cash investment is any type of account that allows you to hold money in a place where you can get to it quickly and easily if you need it, without losing money as a result of "cashing it in" on short notice. This is where you keep the cash reserves we talked about in Chapter 4, "Essential First Steps," on page 45. If you lose your job, or can't work because you smash your hand while out mountain biking, you need easy access to your emergency fund of three to six months' living expenses. Cash investments give you that kind of liquidity. They're also a way to hold funds for any large expenditures you know are coming up in the next year or two, like college tuition, a honeymoon, or a new car to replace that puddle jumper you've been driving. The key is to be able to access the funds without paying a penalty, incurring unnecessary tax liability, or disrupting your long-term investment strategy.

But the need for easy access doesn't mean you have to store dollar bills under your mattress. There are investment vehicles that keep your money relatively safe and provide some return on those dollars, while still allowing you to get your hands on the cash when you need to. Actually, some people say these really aren't investments at all, but just a place to store money. That may or not be the case...but it doesn't really matter. What does matter is how your money works for you. In this case, easy access is the priority. If you can get a small return on the account as well, so much the better.

Here are a few examples of cash investments:

- **Checking account.** I know, you probably don't think of this as an investment. There was a time when some banks actually paid interest on checking accounts, but those have pretty much gone the way of the electric typewriter. As far as liquidity is concerned, though, a checking account is the next best thing to having dollar bills in your pocket. As long as you're not paying a fee for your checking account, it's a good place to store money you'll need to spend in the immediate future. (If you're paying a fee for your checking account, that's like tossing money out the window. It's completely unnecessary. Start shopping today for a no-fee alternative. They're out there.)

- **Savings account.** A savings account is only slightly less accessible than a checking account, especially if you have both in the same financial institution. Accessing the funds is just a matter of transferring money from savings to checking. Still, it's a good way to separate funds you want to hold on to from the money you use for routine expenses. Psychologically, at least, a savings account creates a bit of a firewall between the two. And some banks or credit unions may even pay you a minimal interest on your savings.

- **Money market account.** In most cases this is functionally as liquid as a savings account, but it sometimes requires a higher minimum balance in exchange for a slightly higher interest rate. So if your balance drops below that minimum when you withdraw cash, you could incur a small loss. But that "slightly higher interest rate" is still tiny, so any loss would be minimal. In any case, the return won't keep up with inflation, so it's strictly a way to store money for easy access.

- **Short-term certificate of deposit, or CD.** In this case you do lose access to your money, but only for a short period of time. Basically you hand your money over to a bank for a year or less, maybe as little as three or six months. In return the bank promises to pay you a specific amount of interest when that time is up. Essentially a CD is a loan, only in this case *you're* loaning money *to the bank*. (Nice switch, isn't it?) The interest the bank pays you is minimal (still not enough to keep up with inflation), but it's likely to be a bit higher than a savings or money market account. And with a short-term CD, you do have access to your money within a few months if you need it. (If push comes to shove, you can even cash in a CD before the term is up, but you'll pay a penalty if you do.) This can be a good way to set money aside for that big expense coming up in six months or so.

- **Treasury bill, or T-bill.** This is also a loan, but now you're loaning money to the government for a fixed rate of interest and for a fixed period of time, usually nine months or less. Once again the amount of interest you'll earn is small, but it's more than you'll get storing dollars under the mattress. And remember, the key here is accessibility. Treasury bills provide that, since you hold a T-bill for a relatively short period of time.

EQUITY INVESTMENTS OR "OWNERSHIP"

Anything you own can be considered an "equity" asset, which is just another name for something you own. Your home is an example, because (hopefully) it's worth more than what you owe on it. The difference between your home's market value and the total amount of your mortgage is your equity, because that dollar amount represents the amount of money that would be yours if you sold the home.

Another type of equity asset is stock, as in the kind you buy in the stock market. When you own stock in a company, you own a piece of that company, albeit a tiny piece. For example, if you own 100 shares of Apple stock, you own 0.0000017% of Apple.[18]

The value of a share of stock in any given company fluctuates depending on how much demand there is for it from other investors. If there are more people who want to buy shares in the company than there are people who want to sell shares, demand is high, so the price of a single share goes up. On the other hand, if lots of people want to sell their shares in the company, but few want to buy them, the value of those shares goes down. It's the law of supply and demand in action.

What makes investors want to buy or sell? That's where it gets complicated (which is why you *don't* want to try to guess which way things will go). You might expect it's all about whether the company is making a profit or losing money—but that's just one small piece of the puzzle. If the company has a change in management, investors

---

[18] As of this writing.

might get jittery and rush to sell their shares. Or they might go on a buying spree based on a report that a particular industry is expected to see a growth spurt. Trends that affect a particular market sector—or even the stock market as a whole—can actually override the sales performance of any given company in terms of influence on the price of its shares.

If all of that makes you a little gun shy about trying to figure out which stocks are safe to buy, it should. But that doesn't mean you should stay away from the market altogether. There are tried and true ways you can insulate yourself from much of its volatility, so you can minimize your risk while taking advantage of the opportunity for a good expected return on your long-term investments. I'll explain exactly how to do that in Chapter 8, "Diversify Your Investments for a Safer and More Profitable Journey." For now, what's most important is that you understand the types of investments that are available to you—including the various types of stocks.

Different types of companies = different types of stocks

There are primarily five different types of companies you can invest in.

- **Large companies**, also called large "cap," which is short for "capitalization," a term derived from the amount of "capital," or money, the company is worth on the stock market. The bigger companies have a larger market cap, or capitalization. It's all based on the value of a share of the company's stock multiplied by the number of shares held by shareholders. For example, Apple has roughly 5.7 billion shares held by shareholders...give or take. If a single share was selling at $100, the market cap would be $570 billion. There are different definitions of how large that number has to be before a company's stock is considered "large cap," but generally anything over $5 billion qualifies.

- **Small companies**, or small-cap stocks. Again there are different definitions of how small is "small," but a good rule of thumb is that a small company has a market capitalization of between $300 million and $2 billion. (A company with a capitalization between $2 billion and $5 billion, roughly, would be mid cap; smaller than $300 million would be micro cap. But at this stage of your life as an investor, I wouldn't worry much about those. As long as you have a working understanding of large- and small-cap companies, you're good to go.)

- **Growth companies.** As a general rule, these are companies that are growing, as the name implies. They pay little or no dividend (see "Value companies," below) because they plow their profits back into the company so they can grow in sales volume, diversify their operations, or grow the company in some other way. It can be exciting to see a stock you own flourish as the company releases new products or reports a big increase in sales volume. The advantage to you as an investor is that, as the company grows, the value of your stock will grow along with it—in theory, anyway (there are risks here, but more about that later). Apple is a good example of a growth company.

- **Value companies.** If you invest in this type of stock, when the company does well you can expect to earn a dividend—that's an actual cash payment from the company to its stockholders, usually paid every three months. Value companies are generally not as sexy as growth companies…we're talking utility companies, ball bearing manufacturers, things like that. Oklahoma Gas & Electric Company is an example. You're not likely to see the steady growth in a value company, like you'd expect in a growth company, so chances are there will be less of an increase in the value of your shares over the long term. But value stocks also tend to be more volatile than growth stocks—that means the value of the shares you own is more likely to fluctuate in the short term. In other words, your equity can increase dramatically. That's exciting. But it can also decrease dramatically. And as with any type of stock, if the value of your shares decreases you can end up losing some—or even all—of the money you invested in the first place. Not so exciting.

- **International companies.** Up to now we've been talking primarily about companies owned and operated here in the United States. But you can also buy shares in companies located in other countries. There are stocks available from developed countries like Japan, Germany, and England, and also from less developed countries, what we call "emerging markets," like South Korea and Mexico. International stocks tend to be more volatile (that is, the value fluctuates more dramatically) than stocks from U.S. companies, and emerging market stocks are generally the most volatile over time.

Why do all these distinctions matter to you? Why would you take a chance on more volatile stocks when you can buy something more stable? And why not put all your money into those exciting growth stocks and let it grow along with those hot new companies?

It's all about something we call "diversification," one of the most important strategies you'll use as an investor—so important, in fact, that we'll spend all of Chapter 8 exploring it. For now, let me just say that diversification means you'll spread your money around into all these different types of stocks as a way to protect yourself from the risks every investor faces. As you know, the stock market can go up—and it can go down. But on any given day, some stocks go up while others go down. Often, when large companies are doing well, the small ones are not—and vice versa. The same is true of growth stocks and value stocks—they often move in opposite directions at any given time. If you own a lot of different kinds of stocks, the ones that are going up will help minimize your losses from those that are going down, and optimize your chances for success. And if you also buy the other types of investments we'll talk about in this chapter, you'll be even more successful. You just need to know which types of investments to buy, and how much of your money to put in each one. By the end of Chapter 8, you'll will.

Fixed Investments or "Loanership"

A fixed investment is basically a loan, and you are the lender: You loan a "fixed" amount of money for a "fixed" amount of time. A loan, or debt, usually involves an agreement stating the timely payment of interest and principal. There are a variety of ways you can invest your money this way by loaning it to a bank, a government, or a business, with an agreement that your principal will be returned to you after a predetermined length of time, along with a predetermined amount of interest. We saw how this works with short-term CDs and Treasury bills on page 92.

However, while all CDs are technically a loan in this sense, we generally consider short-term CDs to be cash reserves, because you can access your money in a short period of time. On the other hand, a CD with a term of a year or more is a longer-term investment, and we include those in the category of a fixed, or debt, investment.

Similarly, a Treasury bill is a type of investment known as a "bond"—but as a short-term bond we put it in the category of cash reserves. You can buy longer-term bonds that become part of your long-term investment portfolio, also within the category of a fixed investment.

There are three factors to consider when you purchase a bond (or, if you will, when you loan out your money):

- the entity that issues it,
- its quality, or grade, and
- its term, or the length of time until maturity.

The entity that issues it. The issuing entity is basically the entity you're loaning your money to. Some bonds are issued by the government—the federal government, a state, or a local municipality (like a city or county). The latter are called municipal bonds, or "muni" bonds. The federal government bonds are usually exempt from state taxes, and the muni bonds are tax free on the federal level—sometimes also at the state level. All are backed by the entity that issues them, so federal government bonds are very safe from default. (At least we hope so!) Muni bonds tend to be safe also, but there have been some that have defaulted. Obviously that's not something you want to learn about first hand, so if you are investing in individual muni bonds, it's always good to check out their grade...more about that in a sec.

Corporations can also issue bonds. Your earnings on corporate bonds are taxable on both the state and federal levels. All things being equal (of course they are never exactly equal), corporate bonds pay a higher interest rate than municipal bonds.

The quality or grade of the bond. If the entity that issues a bond suffers a financial crisis or collapse, it may not be able to repay the loan—in other words, it might default on that loan. That means the bond you're holding could become worthless. All bonds are graded for how likely it is they'll default, or their "default risk." There are organizations that provide a grade, or rating, for bonds. Standard & Poor's is one you've probably heard of; Moody's is another. What you need to know here is that there are investment quality bonds and there are "junk" bonds. Now, they don't officially call them junk bonds (that would be a marketing nightmare). So they call them things like "high yield" bonds (doesn't that sound better?), because they pay a high yield, or interest rate—because you run a higher risk of losing all the money you invest, so the opportunity to get that higher yield is an enticement to buy into them despite the risk.

If you include bonds among your investments, it's a good idea to mix some high yield in with your high quality bonds, for reasons we'll discuss in Chapter 8, "Diversify Your Investments for a Safer and More Profitable Journey."

Maturity. We've talked about Treasury bills as a government loan with a very short term, usually nine months or less. With that short of a term, we consider those as part of your cash investments, as we discussed on page 92. But when you're building the debt portion of your portfolio, you might consider including short-term bonds with terms as long as three years. Since you may incur a loss if you sell quickly, they're not considered a cash investment. There are also long-term bonds, which mature in seven years or more. Bonds that mature in three to seven years are what we call "intermediate-term" bonds. It's all based on the length of time until the bond "matures" and pays out the principal amount of money you loaned to the entity issuing it. Regardless of the maturity, most bonds send you a check for your interest (or just credit your account) every six months.

How Much Money Should You Place in Each Type of Investment?

Now that you understand the three basic types of investments, the obvious question is how much to put where. You know that cash investments yield a very small return, so you'll use those just for your cash reserve—an amount equal to three to six months of living expenses.

But what about stocks and bonds? Should you choose one or the other? Or maybe split your money 50:50 between the two?

We'll go into some detail about how to set up a great portfolio when we get to Chapter 14, "Your More than a Millionaire Portfolio," so you'll know just how to allocate money into the different types of investments. For now, let's just say that most, if not all, of your investment dollars should be in stocks. Bonds are a great way to balance your investments in stocks, because those two types of investments differ in the amount of return they offer and in the amount of risk you take when you invest in them. We'll get into the nitty-gritty about risk in Chapter 7.

For now I'll just say that, as an investment category, stocks represent the more volatile portion of your portfolio, which means they come with a greater degree of risk. Bonds carry less risk than stocks, but they also tend to pay a lower return over time. Also, the risk associated with stocks is a greater concern for a short-term investor, like someone who plans to retire in a couple of years, than for a long-term investor. So for someone like you—someone who has 25 years or more to ride out the ups and downs of the market and to accumulate returns—it makes sense to put most or all of your money (80% or more) into stocks, where you have a much greater chance of earning the kind of returns that will help you become More than a Millionaire.

Each of the different types of investments we've talked about in this chapter offer you a different way to earn money and build your wealth. But as you know, all that wealth building does come with a certain amount of risk. You could lose all of the money you invest, or just not earn as much as you expect, or a host of possibilities in between.

The type of risk you incur varies for each type of investment, and we'll explore each one in the next chapter. Even better, I'll follow that with everything you need to know about diversification—it's a powerful strategy you can apply that will go a long way toward minimizing each and every type of risk. Turn the page and you'll see exactly what kind of pitfalls you're up against as an investor, and then learn how to avoid those pitfalls and cut a clear path toward becoming More than a Millionaire.

CHAPTER 7

$↕ WHAT ARE THE RISKS?

So far we've looked at a variety of ways to invest your money. Each one offers a different kind of benefit to you, and covers a different part of your path toward becoming More than a Millionaire. But each type of investment also carries an element of risk. That doesn't mean you shouldn't invest. On the contrary, some would say that not investing at all involves the greatest risk.

The best news here is that investment risk is manageable. There are ways to build enough protection into your strategy that you can venture forward with confidence that you have stacked the odds very much in favor of success. The key is to become familiar with the different kinds of risks and learn the best strategies to minimize them. That's what this chapter is all about.

LOOKING DANGER IN THE EYE

There are many kinds of risks in the world of investing, but there are four that are most common:

- **Inflation risk:** The interest, dividend, or other return you earn on your principle is so small it doesn't keep pace with inflation, so the value of your dollars decreases over time.

- **Business risk**, also called **default risk:** The business, financial institution, or government entity you invest in goes out of business, or defaults, or suffers such a huge loss in value that, when you want to take your money out, you can't get as much back as you put in. It might even mean you lose *all* the money you put in.

- **Market risk:** Even though the individual entity you invested in is doing relatively well, the value of that *type* of investment, as a broad, market stroke, goes down. It's a little bit like paddling a boat upstream. You can't keep up. So the value of your investment is lower when you want your cash back than it was when you put your cash in—you actually have fewer dollars than you put in.

- **Interest rate risk:** You invest in an instrument that pays a specific rate of interest over an extended period of time, and during that time interest rates in general go up. So if you want to sell that instrument, it's less attractive to other buyers because they can get a higher interest rate elsewhere. That means the value of the instrument you own goes down.

Now let's take a look at the three types of investments we reviewed in Chapter 6, and the type of risk you'll face with each one.

Cash investments

When you think of putting your money into a checking, savings, or money market account, or in a CD, it seems pretty darn safe, doesn't it? The account pays a small (I prefer to call it tiny) amount of interest, and you feel confident your cash will be there when you go looking for it. And you're right...mostly. Those bank accounts are all protected by the Federal Deposit Insurance Corporation—you probably know it as FDIC—which insures your money up to a certain amount, currently $250,000 per account holder, per bank. Most credit unions are insured by a similar federal agency called the National Credit Union Administration, or NCUA (if yours is, you'll see the NCUA sticker everywhere). So even if your FDIC backed bank or NCUA backed credit union were to go into default, you'd still be able to retrieve your money (within the limits, of course).

But while it's unlikely you'd lose the money you deposit in a bank account or CD, you do stand to suffer a loss due to **inflation risk**. It's something that's often overlooked by people who choose investments like this as the ultimate safety net. The reality is that, while the actual dollar amount of your principle investment is likely to be there when you need it, the *spendable* value of those dollars probably will not. That's because the amount of interest you earn on your money market or CD is likely to be considerably less than the inflation rate. So if you earn 1% interest, but the cost of living goes up by 2%,[19] you've effectively *lost* 1% of the spendable value of that account.

---

[19] We're using some simplistic numbers here for the sake of illustration. Your actual interest and inflation rates are likely to be different, but the outcome will be similar.

The same is true for Treasury bills. Since buying a T-bill is essentially loaning money to the U.S. government, and we all feel pretty confident Uncle Sam is good for the loan, the dollars you invest will likely be there when you need them. But it's another investment that pays a minimal amount of interest, so you run a substantial risk that the interest you earn will fall far short of inflation. That means your dollars will buy less when you take them out of the account than when you put them in.

Equity investments

When you own stock in a company, you have two ways of earning money on your investment:

- when the company pays you dividends (usually paid quarterly), and
- when the price of the stock increases so that you can sell your shares for more than you paid for them.
- But you also have two ways of running into trouble, because stock ownership carries two different kinds of risk:
- **Business risk**, which means the company does poorly. That can happen because of a drop in sales, or the profit margin might disappear, or the business might even lose money. Or the business can fail completely, and the value of your stock could fall to zero.
- **Market risk**, which means the price of a share of stock in a company falls when the market in general goes down. That can happen even if the company itself is doing well. The

value of its stocks can fall just because more investors suddenly start selling rather than buying the stock, whether because of a national news story that scares them away, a world event, or maybe investors' confidence in the economy drops (for whatever reason, real or perceived). If the market overall is going down, a company's stock price is like a canoe trying to row upstream. Tough to do.

If either of these scenarios occurs, you could earn substantially less than you were hoping for. But even worse, you could lose some or all of the money you invested in the first place.

Fixed investments

The beauty of a fixed investment is that your interest rate is fixed for as long as you hold it. When you put your money into a bond, you know exactly how much you'll earn.

Or do you?

The answer is...probably, but it's not quite that simple. There's still that pesky element of risk to consider. And with fixed investments you have two types of risk to watch out for.

First, the value of any bond you hold is subject to **interest rate risk**. If interest rates go up before the bond matures, its value essentially goes down. Here's why.

Remember, when you buy a bond you agree to a pre-determined interest rate. Let's say you have a $1,000 bond with a ten-year maturity, paying 3% interest. If you hold the bond until it matures, you collect your interest payment every six months, then get your

$1,000 back when the ten-year term is up. But let's say five years into that ten-year term you unexpectedly need cash, and want to sell your bond. Interest rates have gone up, and investors can now get a $1,000 bond paying 4%. Is anyone going to buy your 3% bond if they can get one at 4%? Not a chance. So what do you have to do to sell your 3% bond? Lower your price, perhaps down to $900. (The actual amount would depend on a variety of factors, including the quality of the bond, its maturity, and other market factors.)

That's why when interest rates go up, the value of any bonds you hold goes down—it's interest rate risk in action. The longer the maturity, or term, of your bond the more interest rate risk you assume, because there's a greater opportunity for interest rates to increase before the bond matures.

The reverse is also true. If interest rates go down, the value of your bonds goes up. But there's no way to know ahead of time whether those rates will go up or down.

And of course, bonds also come with **default risk**. Remember, a fixed investment involves "loanership"—you loan money to the entity issuing the bond. If that entity goes out of business, or files for bankruptcy, or otherwise loses value, it might default on your loan and fail to pay back your loan *and* your interest. That's right...you could lose all your money.

Before you toss this book aside and decide to hide all your money under your mattress, remember that understanding your risk is just the first step in minimizing it. For example, when you remember that bonds come with default risk, you'll be sure to minimize that risk by investing in companies or government entities that have solid credit ratings. And that's just one strategy. There are many more, and they're powerful enough to bring your risk down to a very manageable level—and at the same time maximize your opportunity for success.

Let me show you how.

CHAPTER 8

DIVERSIFY YOUR INVESTMENTS FOR A SAFER AND MORE PROFITABLE JOURNEY

We've taken a cold hard look at the risks you face with any investment you choose, and that's important—after all, knowledge is power. The fact that you're still with me says you have the good sense not to let the challenges prevent you from finding solutions. And without a doubt, there are excellent solutions that will nearly eliminate those risks, if you carefully follow the guidelines I'm about to show you.

Don't get me wrong—there are no guarantees. It's been said there is no such thing as a free lunch. That's a pretty good rule of thumb. But when it comes to investing, there's a strategy that lets you get pretty darn close to a free lunch, in that it allows you to minimize much of your risk without forgoing the opportunity to expect a reasonable investment return.

That strategy is called "diversification." In a nutshell, it means you put your money into a diverse array of investment vehicles, so that when some perform poorly in any given time frame (and some will...it's inevitable), others will likely do well enough to keep you on track.

How does it work? The long answer to that question could fill a book much bigger than this one (and there are many books out there that prove my point). But it doesn't have to be that complicated. In just a few pages here I'll show you three simple steps you can take to apply the principles of diversification—three steps that will keep you on a clear path to financial security.

1. First I'll show you how to eliminate the scariest type of risk—that's business risk, the dreaded scenario of a business (or government body) collapsing along with your investment in it.

2. Then I'll explain how to apply strategies that will give you a *higher* expected return along with a *lower* expected risk from other types of losses than the average investor faces.

3. Finally, we'll explore how you can use time to your advantage to lower your risk even further, just by taking a long-term approach to securing your financial future.

STEP ONE:
ELIMINATE BUSINESS RISK

Let's start by getting rid of your biggest nightmare: business risk. That is, you buy stock in a business and the business fails, so you lose your money. Quite possibly *all* your money.

You can eliminate business risk with the first step in your diversification strategy, by spreading your money around into investments that perform differently—some perform well, others not so well. Of course, you don't know at the outset which ones will perform well over the next several years and which ones will tank. But guess what—it doesn't really matter. Perhaps it's best explained with an example.

I'm going to give you two choices of how to invest $100,000 for the next 30 years. I'm even going to tell you ahead of time how both investments will perform. (I know, you don't get that advantage out there in the real world. But heck...I'm that kind of guy.)

- Let's call the first investment "Safe & Steady." It's going to earn a guaranteed 6% annual return. (Don't worry about whether you can actually find an investment that will do that. This is just for illustration purposes.) So if you choose this investment, you'll put the entire $100,000 into Safe & Steady and earn 6% each year for 30 years, without risk. You're a happy camper.

- We'll call the second investment "Thorns & Roses." (It has both thorns and roses...so to speak.) You split your $100,000 into five different bundles, and invest each one in a different way, as follows:

  o You take the first $20,000 to Vegas. (Yep, we're living dangerously here.) Contrary to the claims of all your friends who tell you they made money in Vegas (or, at worst, broke even), you lose it all.

- o You bury the second $20,000 in the back yard. Probably not the best investment, but you know it's going to be there when you go looking for it 30 years down the road.
- o Next you put $20,000 in a certificate of deposit earning 3.0% a year. (As above, this interest rate and all the rates in this example are for illustrative purposes only.)
- o The fourth $20,000 goes into a nice little investment earning an average of 6.0% a year (kind of like our Safe & Steady option above).
- o And the last $20,000 does really well in the stock market. You find a nice growth stock that earns an average of 12% for our 30-year test period.

So that's it:

- $100,000 in your Safe & Steady investment with a guaranteed 6%, or
- $100,000 in your Thorns & Roses investment plan, but you split it into chunks of $20,000 in each of five choices, with only one of those doing better than the guaranteed 6%.

Which one would you choose? Does it feel like a trick question? I've posed the question to hundreds of people over the years—most of them CPAs—and more than 95% choose the Safe & Steady investment. How about you?

Let's take a look at how both options performed.

First, the most popular choice:

Safe & Steady		
Amount	Average annual return[20]	Value in 30 years
$100,000	6%	$574,349

After 30 years your Safe & Steady investment would be worth $574,349. Not bad.

Now let's break down the Thorns & Roses investment.

Thorns & Roses			
Amount	Investment choice	Average annual return[21]	Value in 30 years
$20,000	Vegas	Lost it all in one trip	$ 0
$20,000	Bury it in the yard	0%	$ 20,000
$20,000	Certificate of deposit	3%	$ 48,545
$20,000	Safe & Steady investment	6%	$114,870
$20,000	Hot stock	12%	$599,198
Total:			$782,613

That's right—after 30 years you'd end up with $782,613, or $208,264 more than if you'd put all your money in the safe bet.

---

[20] This is just a mathematical example offered as an illustration, and does not suggest any type of investment vehicle. Even if it did, as I often say, past performance is no guarantee of future performance.
[21] This is just a mathematical example offered as an illustration, and does not suggest any type of investment vehicle. Even if it did, as I often say, past performance is no guarantee of future performance.

That's a 36% greater return on your money when you spread it out, or *diversify* your investment. And since we know you're too smart to blow $20,000 in Las Vegas, just think how well you could have done!

But what if you'd put it all into that hot stock that earned 12%? Well, sure, that'd be great. But there's no way to know for sure which stock will do that, especially in the long years between now and the day you retire. You can try to pick the next Apple but, remember, this is all about avoiding business risk. If that stock that looks so great now ends up going belly up in 20 years, you'll lose a huge chunk of your retirement fund. If you spread it all around, you'll protect yourself from business risk and benefit from the Thorns & Roses strategy—a.k.a. diversification.

A better way to diversify

You've seen the impact of spreading your money around into just five different investments rather than just one. But in reality you should diversify into more than five investments. (And we don't even need to talk about Vegas, do we?) If investing in five different vehicles is good, imagine what 20 or 30 or 100 would do. If finding that many different companies to buy stock in seems as tough as climbing a small mountain, never fear.

One of the best ways to minimize business risk through diversification is by buying mutual funds. A mutual fund is an investment tool in which thousands of individuals, like yourself, pool their money and let a professional money manager select, manage, and sell investments on their behalf. The beauty of a mutual fund is that a single fund invests in many different businesses—so many, in fact, that it virtually eliminates business risk. If one of the businesses held by the mutual fund goes bankrupt, there are many businesses within that fund to cushion the blow.

The trade-off with mutual funds is that you lose the chance for the big home run that might come from investing all your money in the next hot stock. Then again, you won't get wiped out by investing in the wrong stock (or a few wrong stocks) and losing everything when it goes under. This is how you virtually eliminate business risk in Step One of our diversification strategy.

You can invest in a mutual fund with a very modest amount of money. You can do it on a monthly basis or buy in with a lump sum. If you're investing through your company's retirement plan, you can start with as little as $25 a month. But even if you're managing your retirement fund on your own, many mutual funds will let you start with a $1000 initial amount, and then you can add to it in increments of as little as $25.

Mutual funds offer many advantages, including:

- Professional management: Each fund is administered by a professional who is an expert investor. He or she is responsible for deciding which stocks to buy for the fund, and for monitoring its performance over time. The fund manager evaluates each stock, or business, for a variety of factors that determine whether it has the potential to perform well for you and the thousands of other people invested in the fund.

- The power of diversification: You've seen how powerful it can be to spread your money around among a handful of different investments. With a single share of a mutual fund, you automatically spread your money among twenty or a hundred or more different stocks. You virtually eliminate that business risk we've talked about, and have an opportunity to increase your returns substantially.

- Continuous monitoring: Do you want to spend an hour or two or six every day monitoring the performance of each of your stocks? Do you have time to read the business news every day to keep an eye out for a serious downturn in one of those company's earnings? Or would you rather spend your free time out hiking that trail down by the river? A mutual fund comes complete with an expert on the job to keep an eye on things. That doesn't mean you can ignore your portfolio and its performance—but it does mean you can leave the day-to-day details to someone with many years of experience managing investments.

- Being part of an investment pool: How many different stocks could you buy with an initial $25 investment, or even $1,000? You'd be lucky to buy one highly rated share. When you pool your money with other investors, as you do in a mutual fund, you get the benefit of broad diversification with a very small investment. There's truly no other way to get that much bang for your buck.

Okay, I can see you're convinced. So where do you find a mutual fund to buy? There are literally thousands to choose from, and there are many ways for you to research which ones are best for you.[22] There are probably several available through your retirement account at work, if you have one. If not, let me get you started by pointing you to a group of funds offered by an investment firm called Vanguard. You can find it at www.Vanguard.com.

As for our Safe & Steady versus Thorns & Roses experiment...you may not have $100,000 now, but you will if you are disciplined and follow the principles outlined in these chapters. Even if you are just starting out investing $25 dollars per month, these diversification strategies work the same. Now let's move on to Step Two.

STEP TWO:
OFFSET YOUR LOSSES

Now that you understand how to start diversifying by putting your money into mutual funds, you're ready to take Step Two—you might say it's a way to diversify your diversification. Just as you use a mutual fund to put your money into many different stocks, you can take that diversification to the next level by putting money into several different mutual funds. There's even a strategy that lets you choose funds that are likely to perform differently at any given time—that is, when one loses money another will gain. That strategy is called "asset allocation." Just as we saw in Step One, by taking the

---

[22] You can begin by exploring the many resources at www.Morningstar.com.

principles of diversification a step further you'll do an even better job of increasing your expected return and decreasing your risk.

First let's look at a very simple example of two businesses that perform differently, and then we'll apply what we learn to mutual funds. Here goes.

Let's start with a fictional business—we'll call it SummerSports. It sells summertime sporting items like swimwear, sandals, ski boats...things like that. Its sales do really well...in the summer months. Sales over a year look like this:

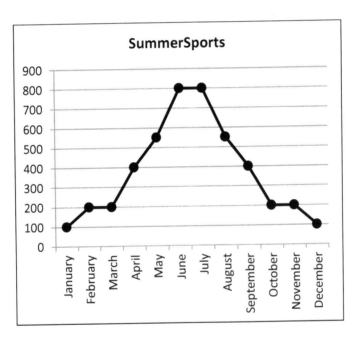

Now let's look at a business of a different type. We'll call this one Wintersports, because it sells things you'd use in the wintertime—toboggans, gear for snow skiing, and maybe snowmobiles. The sales numbers are exceptionally good...in the winter. Over a typical year, sales look like this:

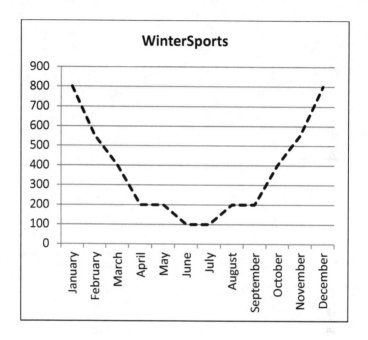

As you can see, sales for both businesses have large swings up and down.

Now let's say you've got an itch to get into the sporting goods business, but you don't really like wide variations in sales volume, so what do you do? Simple. You buy both of the companies in our example, SummerSports and WinterSports. You hold both companies as subsidiaries of a single parent company...let's call it All Seasons Sports. Now your overall sales figures look like this:

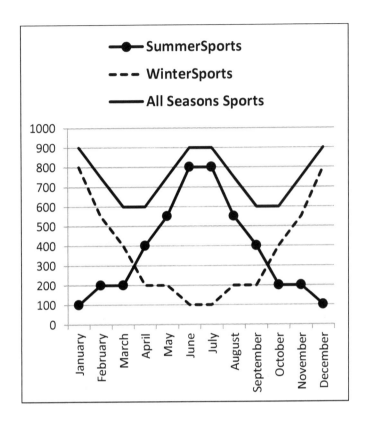

This is counterintuitive. (At least it was for me at first). You took two volatile businesses, but the combination is *less volatile than either of the parts.*

This is what happens when you apply Step Two of our diversification strategy. Your two volatile businesses moved in different directions—when one was going down, the other was going up. When it was cold and snowy outside, people were talking and thinking about winter sports equipment—"That fancy new high-tech snowboard is in!"—so the sales figures for WinterSports soared. At the same time, however, SummerSports' sales were in the tank. After all, who thinks about swimwear in the winter? During the summer months, the exact opposite was true. SummerSports' sales were strong, while WinterSports' sales were not. But you're sitting pretty, because you were smart enough to buy *both* companies, and the volatility in each was balanced by the other.

The same principle applies to stocks and mutual funds. Just like our fictional sporting goods companies, different types of mutual funds move differently at any given time, or in any given financial climate. By blending them properly, the sum of the parts can be better than each component, even when that component, in and of itself, is volatile.

With this being said, things are never quite as cut and dried in the investment world as they were for our SummerSports and WinterSports businesses. But in a well-planned portfolio you blend many different types of investments, called "asset classes," that are likely to move in different directions in different types of economic situations. Just as our SummerSports and WinterSports companies sales performed differently in our example, mutual funds that consist of large companies might perform differently from small companies under a particular set of circumstances; stocks in United States companies would likely behave differently from international stocks or intermediate-term bonds. There are plenty of other examples, but I think the point is clear: Diversify, my friend. Diversify.

As it turns out, you don't have to diversify into hundreds of different mutual funds. Choosing between five and nine quality funds should work well for you. By choosing the right balance of asset classes, you can, over time, get the best expected return for the given level of risk for your goals and time frame. In Chapter 14, "Your More than a Millionaire Portfolio," I'll show you an example of a well-balanced portfolio that will do that for you.

Step Three:
Let Time Work in Your Favor

Once you've diversified your investments using mutual funds, and taken the added step of buying mutual funds from different asset classes, it's time to look at how you can use time to increase the power of diversification even more. By carefully planning when you invest your money and when you take it out, you can reduce your risk and increase your returns even more.

As you can imagine, we have mountains of data that tell us how a given investment is likely to perform in a particular scenario. That doesn't mean we can predict what a single stock or mutual fund will do in a given year. (If anyone tells you they can, turn around and head for the hills.) But we can definitely identify long-term trends and averages, and we can look at the highs and lows of how a particular type of investment has performed over a given period of time.

For example, we know that in any single year, a well-diversified portfolio that's made up of 100% stocks (no bonds, CDs, or anything else) is likely to perform within a certain range of gains and losses. On the high side, in any one year, that diversified portfolio of 100% stocks could give you a return as high as 30%; on the low side it's likely to lose 15%.[23] In other words, if you have all your money into a nicely diversified assortment of stocks, your return will be somewhere between a gain of 30% and a loss of 15%. Sounds pretty risky, doesn't it? Even worse, with this type of portfolio you should expect that, over a ten-year time frame, you'll have two or maybe even three negative years. (And wouldn't it be great if I knew which years they were? Sorry, I don't.)

But here's what's magical. Over time, the good years and bad start to even out. What is amazing, at least to me, is this: In a ten-year time frame, the high end of your potential earnings is only 16%.[24] I know, that's a big drop from the one-year number. But here's the good part: The low end of that range of your potential return is a *gain* of 3%![25] That's right, it's a *gain*, not a loss! The worst you can expect to earn, with a very high degree of confidence,[26] is 3%—the risk of loss doesn't completely disappear, but it's very nearly eliminated. And it gets even better: The longer the time frame we look at—or to say it another way, the longer you hold on to your investment—the range between the expected high and low returns continues to collapse around an expected gain of 10%. (That's the

---

[23] With 95% confidence. I can't offer a 100% guarantee because earnings can always be higher or lower than these numbers. Most important, past performance is not a guarantee of future performance.
[24] With 95% confidence. I can't offer a 100% guarantee because earnings can always be higher or lower than these numbers. Most important, past performance is not a guarantee of future performance.
[25] With 95% confidence. I can't offer a 100% guarantee because earnings can always be higher or lower than these numbers. Most important, past performance is not a guarantee of future performance.
[26] Again, with 95% confidence.

average of the same ranges we've looked at for your 1-year and 10-year returns.)

Here's another way to look at it:

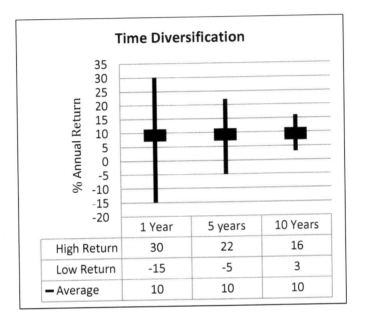

	1 Year	5 years	10 Years
High Return	30	22	16
Low Return	-15	-5	3
— Average	10	10	10

So there you have it. In Step One you diversified away your business risk by spreading your money around into different investments, using mutual funds. In Step Two you saw that investing in different *types* of mutual funds that move in different directions in any given year will reduce your risk and give you a better overall return over time. And in Step Three you discovered how to let diversification do even more for you by investing over a longer time frame, to let the good and the bad years even out so your range of possible returns narrows greatly and reduces your risk.

The takeaway is this: With these three simple steps you can apply decades of data and reams of research to smooth out the bumps and pitfalls on the way to becoming More than a Millionaire. There are no guarantees. But this is the next best thing: a sound strategy to help you map your path to success.

CHAPTER 9

DOLLAR COST AVERAGING: "THE NEXT BEST THING TO GOD TELLING YOU WHEN TO BUY"

"Expect volatility, and profit from it." These wise words are from Benjamin Graham. He was Warren Buffet's mentor, and was one of the greatest investors of all time. In 1949 he wrote *The Intelligent Investor* and, incredibly, it's still considered an important read for anyone who wishes to do an effective job of managing their investments in stocks.

Dollar cost averaging (DCA) is one of many hallmarks of Graham's genius that has stood the test of time.[27] It's one of the best investment strategies for reducing your risk and increasing your potential return in the long term. DCA is such a good strategy that investment advisor Nick Murray calls it "the next best thing to a buy signal from God."

---

[27] Daniel Myers, "Benjamin Graham: Three Timeless Principles," *Forbes*, February 23, 2009, http://www.forbes.com/2009/02/23/graham-buffett-value-personal-finance_benjamin_graham.html, accessed January 5, 2017.

Why is dollar cost averaging so powerful? One of the scariest things for an investor is the prospect of the stock market going down. And the reality is that it *will* go down. But history has shown us that it will eventually go up again. That's volatility—the market fluctuates up and down. It's just the nature of the beast. But DCA allows you to let the volatility of the market work in your favor or, to paraphrase Graham's words, to profit from the market's inevitable volatility. Let me explain how that's possible.

One of the few things you can know for sure as an investor is that, on a *short-term* basis, you can't predict when the market will go up or when it's going to go down. Many have tried, and some succeed now and then. But trust me on this—all have failed in the long run. Sure, there are people who will be happy to gloat about the times they were right. But they're a bit like a gambler who wins big in Las Vegas. You can be sure that over time he'll find himself on the losing end of that wager. There is no single investment strategy that works every time, in the short run, in every situation. The best strategies work well over an extended period of time in a wide variety of scenarios.

Dollar cost averaging is one of those. It works extremely well over the long haul. That's why it's been around a long time, and why it's considered an essential component of a solid investment plan.

WHAT IS IT?

Dollar cost averaging means that you invest the same amount of money again and again on a regular schedule. For example, you might invest $100 into your 401(k) fund every pay period. That money goes into your investment account every two weeks (or twice a month, or monthly, as the case may be). What makes that so powerful is that you're investing when the market is going up—and also when the market is going down. It may seem like a bad idea to invest when the market is going down. But remember, you never know when it's going to start heading upward again. Also, if you invest that $100 when the market is down, you'll be buying more shares because their value is less. Then, when the market does turn around you'll have that many more shares increasing in value—so suddenly that unpredictable, up-and-down volatility of the market is working in your favor...just as Benjamin Graham said it would.

Three different investments: Which one would you pick?

Let's take a look at three different investment vehicles, each with an initial value of $10 per unit (or share), and with each performing differently over a period of five years. Then we'll see what would have happened if you'd put money into each one using the principles of dollar cost averaging.

- Investment #1: It starts at a value of $10 per unit, then increases in value by $2 every year. At the end of year 1 it goes to $12, year 2 to $14, year 3 to $16, and year 4 to $18. At the end of year 5 it's worth $20 per share. It seems obvious that this would have been a great place to put your money every year.

- Investment #2: This one didn't fare quite as well. It started off at $10, then it dropped to $8 after the first year, then

down to $5 in year 2, and stayed at $5 in year 3. In year 4 it
rebounded a bit to $8, and at the end of year 5 it finally
made it back to its starting price at $10. It probably would
seem a bit disheartening to have put your money into an
investment that went down for three years, and after 5 full
years was just back to where it started. Not what you had
hoped for.

- Investment #3. This one was horrible. Starting out at $10, it
went to $7 after a year, then $4 in year 2, all the way down
to $1 in year 3. It stayed at $1 in year 4, then only made it up
to $4 at the end of year 5. Clearly you'd have put your money
into what many would call a disaster.

Here are all three investments and their performances lined up
side by side:

	Price per Unit:		
	Investment #1	Investment #2	Investment #3
Initial investment	$10	$10	$10
Year 1	$12	$8	$7
Year 2	$14	$5	$4
Year 3	$16	$5	$1
Year 4	$18	$8	$1
Year 5	$20	$10	$4

Or, if you prefer, a graph of the three investments:

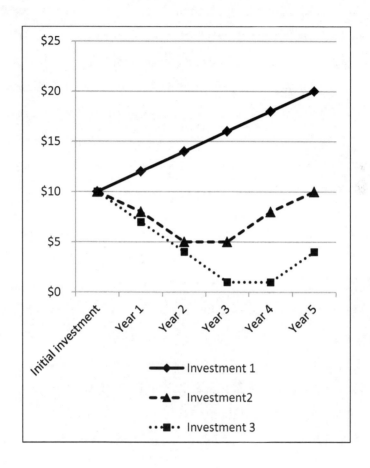

What happens if you apply our dollar cost averaging strategy to each of these investments? Let's say you invest $1,000 each year for five years, then sell at the end of year 5. Which one do you make the most money on? I'll give you a hint: One of them earns you almost 30% more than the other two.

Most people think the obvious choice is Investment #1, since it increases in value each year. But that's almost too obvious, so some guess that Investment #2 is the winner. Here's the big surprise: Dollar cost averaging is so powerful that you can make money even when an investment has done as poorly as Investment #3.

I'll prove it to you. Here are the results of our experiment—the final value of your portfolio after investing a total of $5,000, or $1,000 each year for five years, in each of our three investments:

Investment #1: $8,456

Investment #2: $8,500

Investment #3: $10,971

You didn't see that coming, did you? Only about 1% of the people I talk to see this. Why did Investment #3, which did so poorly year after year, outperform the other two? Not only did it outperform the others, it ended up worth almost 30% more than Investment #1, which did nothing but go up. It was dollar cost averaging that made that happen. Let's take a closer look.

When Investment #3 was at its lowest point, $1 per unit, you invested $1,000 into it, buying 1,000 very cheap units (at $1 per unit). When it bounced a little, to $4, those cheap shares did very, very well. That year's $1,000 essentially quadrupled itself.[28] On the other hand, when Investment #1 was at $18, your $1,000 only bought you 55.56 shares. When the value of those shares went up to $20, your last $1,000 investment only increased by about 11%.

Unfortunately there is a catch. It's one thing for Investment #3 to drop to $1, but you wouldn't want it to go from $1 to zero, which it

---

[28] To be clear, investments almost never quadruple in a year. This is just an illustration of how DCA works.

can if you invest in an individual stock. As you may recall, that's called business risk. The good news is that you can virtually eliminate that kind of risk, as we saw in Chapter 8. That's where diversification comes into play, so that you own hundreds of stocks instead of just one, by buying mutual funds instead of individual stocks. When you're in a mutual fund, if a few of the stocks in the fund go under, you don't care because you have hundreds of others that can make up the difference.

DOLLAR COST AVERAGING
FOR A LONG-TERM INVESTOR—LIKE YOU

This experiment makes it clear why dollar cost averaging works best with investments that fluctuate, and for investors who have an eye on the long term—just like you.

How long is long term? We're talking about the duration of your work career, which I assume is likely to be 25 to 35 years. (If you expect to work longer than that, that's fine. I want to get you to a point where, if you continue to work longer than that, it's because you want to—not because you have to.) However, at a minimum, to reap the benefits of dollar cost averaging your investment objective needs to be at least 7 to 10 years, and preferably at least 15 years. Fifteen years is a good target because the stock market has never seen a negative result over a 15-year time frame since we've been keeping track, which is since 1934. That's not to say it hasn't seen some volatile times. And of course, past performance is not a guarantee of future results. But I'd say a track record that runs that long is a pretty reliable one.

Here's a case in point. Many investors talk about how bad the period from 2000 to 2002 was for the stock market. Or perhaps you'd rather talk about 2008, the second worst year since 1815 for large companies.[29] But if you had invested $1,000 a year—applying dollar cost averaging, of course—starting at the beginning of 2000 (a horrible time to start!), and continued for 15 years until 2014, you would have invested a total of $15,000. If you had sold your portfolio at the end of 2014, your investment would have been worth $29,817.[30] That's the power of dollar cost averaging for a long-term investor.

Count on it, the market will fluctuate...sometimes wildly. You can reduce some of that volatility through diversification. But rather than fear volatility, let it work to your advantage through dollar cost averaging.

---

[29] Ibbotson SBBI, 2013 Classic Yearbook, 2013, Published by Morningstar, Inc.
[30] Ibbotson SBBI, 2015 Classic Yearbook, 2015, Published by Morningstar, Inc.

CHAPTER 10

 TAX STRATEGiES TO
DOUBLE YOUR RETiREMENT INCOME

It might seem that taxes would be a trivial matter when investing for retirement. I mean, as they say, the only things certain in life are death and taxes. (Please note, though, that death doesn't get worse every time congress meets.) You have to pay Uncle Sam, and that's that...right?

Well...yes and no. It's true that you have to be diligent about paying the taxes you're legally required to pay. Not doing so will not only wreck your financial future, but can easily land you in jail. But the operative phrase here is "legally required to pay." So think in terms of tax avoidance, not tax evasion. The difference? About five years.

Our federal income tax code now consists of more than four million words. That's a good indication of how complex it is—and how intimidating. So most people just bite the bullet, fill out an IRS Form 1040 by April 15, and leave it at that. Whether you have money taken out of your paycheck or write a check on tax day, a substantial portion of your income is gone before you can even think about what to spend it on. Approximately 31% of the nation's income goes to taxes.[31] In fact, Americans spend more on taxes than on food, clothing, and housing...combined.

We can't begin, in this book, to address all the ways you can reduce your tax burden. What we can do is look at how different types of investments are taxed differently. Understanding those differences, and applying them to your investment decisions, can save you plenty of tax dollars now, throughout your years as an investor, and after you retire. In fact, the techniques I'm about to show you are so powerful, they can literally double the amount of money you'll have when you retire. That's no small change.

Pay Taxes Now. Pay Taxes Later—or Not

Let's begin by looking at some of the different ways investment money is taxed. There are lots of different scenarios, but they all boil down to two factors:

- what happens to the money before you invest it—that is, whether you put money into your investment account before taxes are taken out or after they're taken out—and
- what happens to your earnings from your investments—that is, when *or if* you have to pay taxes on the earnings

---

[31] Kyle Pomerleau, "Tax Freedom Day 2015," Tax Foundation Report, March 2015,
http://taxfoundation.org/sites/taxfoundation.org/files/docs/TaxFoundation_TFD_Report.pdf, accessed January 5, 2017.

from your investments. (You read that right. "If" means there are situations in which you never have to pay taxes on your earnings. How cool is that?)

First let's look at what happens to your money before you invest it.

- **After-tax dollars.** This is the simplest way to handle your investment money. It might also be the most costly where taxes are concerned. Your "after-tax dollars" are the dollars you have left *after* taxes are taken out of your paycheck, or *after* you've set aside money for taxes. Whether you literally take the taxes out or not, when April 15 rolls around you're responsible for income tax on all of those dollars—including any money you've put into your investment account.

    For example, if you made $100 and paid in $30 in taxes, you would have $70 of after-tax dollars to invest. And your records will show that you've already paid taxes on those dollars.

- **Before-tax dollars.** There are investment vehicles that allow you to put money into them *before* you pay income tax on it. If you have taxes withheld from your paycheck, you get to put a limited portion of your money into your retirement account, *and then* taxes are calculated and deducted from what's left. If you pay your own taxes, you get to choose how much you want to invest (up to certain limits) *before* you calculate how much tax you have to pay.

In this case, if you make $100, and invest $10 *before taxes* in a retirement account, you would then pay taxes *only* on the $90 that's left. You invested your money *before* taxes.

Now let's look at what happens to your earnings on investments.

- **Pay as you go.** This means you pay taxes on your investment earnings as you earn them. You might include them when you do your taxes on April 15, or your financial services company might withhold taxes for you before they pay you a dividend or capital gain (such as when you sell a stock for more than you paid for it). In any case, those earnings will likely be reported to the IRS on your behalf, just as your ordinary income is.

  Most after-tax investments require you to pay as you go. The amount of tax you pay on your returns can vary quite a lot, depending on the type of investment and the type of earnings. Most dividends are taxed at your normal income tax rate; others are not taxed at all or are subject to a reduced rate, depending on your income. Some capital gains earnings are subject to a lower rate, depending on how long you held the property. Some bonds are subject to federal tax but not state tax, and vice versa. It quickly becomes pretty complicated—and the tax laws change every year.

There's no need to get bogged down in those details at this point. Just be prepared to evaluate any investment vehicle you're considering so you're clear about when the earnings are taxable. Many people say it's best to pay as you go because they expect tax rates to be higher in the future, and they don't want to owe a bundle of taxes at retirement. There's some merit to that position, but it's not the whole story, as you'll see in a minute.

- **Tax deferred.** With some investments you don't need to pay any taxes on your returns until you pull the money from the investment vehicle. Taxes on your yearly gains are *deferred* until you withdraw the principal and earnings, presumably when you retire.

  There are a couple of benefits to this. First, it means you have more money sitting in the investment account earning money for you, rather than filling the coffers of the Treasury Department. The other benefit only comes into play if you're in a lower tax bracket when you retire. Since the tax rate you pay on most returns is tied to your income tax rate, that could amount to a substantial savings.

- **Tax free.** Tax free means tax free. With these investments you don't pay any taxes on your earnings. Ever. In almost all cases these are investments in which you invest after-tax dollars (though not all after-tax investments offer tax-free earnings). The downside is that with after-tax dollars you have, by definition, less dollars to invest. On the other hand, if those investments produce a hefty return, you might tip your hat to Uncle Sam when you're out spending those earnings.

That might seem like a lot to digest, but it all comes down to a few basic points. Sometimes you invest before you pay taxes, sometimes you don't. And sometimes you pay taxes on your earnings as you earn them, sometimes you pay on your earnings when you retire (or otherwise pull money out of the account), and sometimes you get to keep every penny you earn. Every investment you consider should be evaluated for when you pay taxes—on the money you put in *and* on the money you take out. But what are the best options for your situation?

A perfect investment would be before tax and tax free, so you'd never have to pay taxes before you put the money in or after you take it out. Unfortunately, that really doesn't exist at this time.[32] But there are other combinations that can work well for you now and in the long run. Let's look at your three primary choices:

- **After tax and pay as you go.** A basic brokerage account would function this way, as would a CD that isn't in an IRA (more on IRAs in a minute). You use after-tax dollars to buy some investments, and you pay taxes on your earnings as you earn them.

---

[32] Although some 529 plans for college education come close. Many states give you a tax deduction (so you're investing before-state-tax dollars), though you still have to pay *federal* income tax before you invest. But if the funds are used for qualified college expenses, earnings are federal- and state-income-tax free.

- **Before tax and tax deferred.** You probably know that an IRA, or Individual Retirement Account, is a way to set money aside for retirement. In a traditional IRA you invest before-tax dollars into an account, and the earnings on that account grow without being taxed. You pay taxes on your earnings—as well as the amount you originally invested—only when you withdraw the funds. A traditional 401(k), 403(b), and similar accounts function the same way.

- **After tax and tax free.** In 1997, an instrument called the Roth IRA was created to offer an alternative to save for retirement. When you decide to put your money into an account designated as a Roth IRA, you pay your taxes first, then invest after-tax dollars. As long as you comply with the requirements (including leaving your money in the Roth for at least five years and waiting until you're at least 59½ years old), you can pull your money out—including *all* of your earnings—tax free.[33] There are also Roth 401(k) accounts that offer similar options.

WHICH ONE WOULD YOU CHOOSE?

Let's say you have $100 to invest each month for 35 years. And let's assume you're in the 30% tax bracket. You invest in a well-diversified portfolio and, because you've read this book, you've chosen mutual funds. All your mutual funds are in stocks, or equity

---

[33] As always, check with your tax professional. Laws are subject to change without notice and often do.

funds. Your earnings fluctuate, of course, but over time you average a gain of 10% per year.[34]

Let's see how your investment of $100 per month performs under each of the taxation situations we've discussed: after tax and pay as you go, after tax and tax free, and before tax and tax deferred.

- **After tax and pay as you go.** Since you're investing after-tax dollars, and you're in the 30% tax bracket, after you've paid your taxes you're left with $70 to invest. Each month that $70 goes into your portfolio, earning an average of 10% per year, and you pay taxes on those earnings as you earn them. At the end of 35 years you will have about $127,000 dollars with no taxes due.

- **After tax and tax free.** Again you're using after-tax dollars, so your $100 is reduced to $70 invested every month, with a 10% return. At the end of our 35-year time frame you will have about $268,000. Not bad. And if you are 59½ or older when you take the money out, it's tax free. Clearly a better choice than the first one.

- **Before tax and tax deferred.** In this case you get to invest the entire $100 every month because, remember, you're using pre-tax dollars. After 35 years of earning an average 10% annual gain, you would have about $383,000 in your

---

[34] This approximate10% average return is based on the median return from January 1, 1973, to October 31, 2015, modeling a simulated SEI Institutional Equity portfolio using a software modeling system called Advisory World. The median return is actually 10.30%, but to keep our illustration simple I've used 10%. However, keep in mind that past performance does not mean your—or any—portfolio will perform at that level in the future.

portfolio. Of course, all of it is taxable when you take it out. Some people would say this is an awful choice because, if you took it all out at once and you're still in the 30% tax bracket, you'd be left with about $268,000. But who would do that? You get to choose how and when you take your income out of the fund.[35] And if you think you might be in a lower tax bracket when you retire, you could end up keeping more of your money than you would have if you'd paid those taxes during the years when your income is higher.

It's pretty clear these last two choices (after tax and tax free, and before tax and tax deferred) are better than the first option (after tax and pay as you go). Whether you use pre-tax or after-tax dollars, you want to avoid paying taxes on your investment returns as you earn them. Those pay-as-you-go taxes are a huge drain on your earning potential. You're much better off if you can let your earnings earn money for you year after year.

Okay, we've narrowed it down to two options. Which of those is best for you?

It depends on your tax bracket when you start and your tax bracket when you take your money out. I won't bore you with a bunch of mathematical equations or complicated rationale, but I'll give you a few rules of thumb that I use.[36]

---

[35] As a general rule, up until you are 70½ years old you can choose how and when you take money out. When you pass the 70½ mark you're required to take out a certain amount each year. It's called a "required minimum distribution."
[36] Based upon 2016 tax brackets.

If you're single:

- **If your taxable income is less than $10,000 dollars a year**, then after tax and tax free is the way to go, so look for a Roth IRA or Roth 401(k).

- **If your taxable income is greater than $37,500** then the before-tax and tax-deferred option is better. You want a traditional IRA or 401(k) or something similar.

- **If your taxable income is between the $10,000 and $37,500**, then frankly it's a toss-up. I generally prefer the before-tax and tax-deferred option. Seems to me, a tax-saving bird in the hand is worth more than a promise of tax savings many years from now. All things being equal (or unknowable), you might as well have as many of your hard-earned dollars as possible in that portfolio earning money for you.

If you're married and filing jointly:

- **If your taxable income is less than $18,500**, then the after-tax and tax-free option is preferred. Put your money in a Roth IRA.

- **If your income taxable is greater than $75,000**, then I recommend the before-tax and tax-deferred option.

- **If your taxable income is between $18,500 and $75,000**, again it's a toss-up. I prefer before tax and tax deferred.

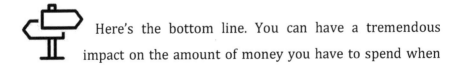 Here's the bottom line. You can have a tremendous impact on the amount of money you have to spend when

you retire, just by holding your portfolio in the right type of account. You can literally double the income you'll have 35 years from now, just by choosing an IRA or 401(k)—traditional or Roth—as your primary investment account. Unfortunately there's a limit to how much money you can put into an IRA and some 401(k) accounts.[37] Once you've maxed out these options for your retirement nest egg, then the pay-as-you-go accounts make sense, but not before.

To make things as simple as possible, here are my recommendations, in order of priority, for how you can get the best tax advantages at this stage in your investment career.[38] When you've maxed out your limits on item #1, start putting money into item #2, and so forth.

1. Put as much as you can into your before-tax 401(k).
2. Put as much as you can into a before-tax traditional IRA
3. Put as much as current tax law allows into a Roth IRA
4. Put as much as your budget allows into a pay-as-you-go account.

The road to becoming More than a Millionaire is shorter and easier if you can reduce the drag of taxes—and you can. By legally avoiding taxes and implementing tax-advantaged investment strategies, you can reach your destination in half the time.

Suddenly the choices look pretty simple, don't they?

---

[37] The limit varies depending on your circumstances, and the law changes from time to time. Check with a tax professional to find out what you can and cannot do.

[38] As always, check with your tax professional. Laws are subject to change without notice and often do.

PART IV

MAKE IT HAPPEN!

CHAPTER 11

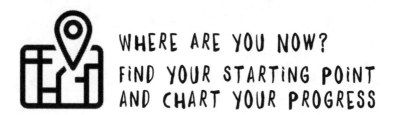

WHERE ARE YOU NOW?
FIND YOUR STARTING POINT
AND CHART YOUR PROGRESS

You *can* become More than a Millionaire. But how will you know when you get there? And how far along on the path are you now? Are you ahead of schedule or behind? Wouldn't it be sad if you were doing great and didn't know it? You might be worrying, and not enjoying the money you have now, for no reason. But how can you be sure it's okay to relax and enjoy a little discretionary spending now and then?

The answer is...you keep score.

In the world of finance, we have a very handy tool to help you keep score at every stage of your journey to building wealth. That tool is called a "net worth statement." It's essentially a tally of how much you have, how much you owe, and a comparison of the two.

In this chapter I'll show you how to create a net worth statement and how to analyze it, so you'll always know exactly how much progress you've made on your path to becoming More than a Millionaire...and how much further you have to go.

Your Net Worth Statement

A net worth statement is a way to gather all the information you need to determine what your "net worth" is—that's the magical number you arrive at when you take the value of all your assets (what you own) and subtract out all of your liabilities (what you owe). Hopefully the result is a positive number. If you're like me, it may be a bit of a stretch to get there. When I created my first net worth statement I included my clothes as assets in hopes of ending up with a positive net worth. I didn't make it.

In a way, your net worth is similar to a spending plan (see Chapter 5, beginning on page 61), in that it allows you to assess how you're doing financially. But the net worth looks at your finances on a given day, while the spending plan monitors them over a period of time. I once heard a financial advisor explain that the net worth is a snapshot, while a spending plan is a movie.

I know that by now you're keeping track of your spending every day. (You are, aren't you?) But how often should you do your net worth statement? In general it's a good idea to do it at least once a year, however at first you may want to do it more often. When you begin implementing your More than a Millionaire strategy you'll see significant, positive changes to your net worth fairly quickly. That will give you motivation to stick with it, and also help you gain a better understanding of how the process works. So for the first couple of years I would suggest you do a net worth statement quarterly, then for a couple of years do it every six months. After that it's probably sufficient to do it annually.

To make it part of your routine, plan to do it on the same day each year—perhaps on the one-year anniversary of the day you start your More than a Millionaire journey.

YOUR NET WORTH WORKSHEET

Generally the net worth statement starts with your assets (what you own), then follows with a list of your liabilities (what you owe), and finally your net worth (what you own minus what you owe). To give you a more complete picture, your assets are usually broken down into several different categories. For our purposes here, we look at the following types of assets:

- Cash
- Investments
- Property

As your wealth increases, your finances are likely to become more complicated, and so your net worth statement may need to be more complex than this. But this simplified approach is a great starting point, and it will take you a long way until you need to enlist the help of a professional financial advisor.

Let's take a closer look at each section of your net worth statement.

Assets (What you own)

Your assets include anything you own that has financial value, from the money in your checking account to your home (if you own it) and its contents (even if you don't) and many things in between. Here are the main categories of assets you should include on your net worth statement.

Cash accounts. Usually your list of assets starts with those that are the most liquid—your cash accounts. In this context, "cash" doesn't just refer to the dollar bills you have in your pocket. It includes the various types of cash accounts we looked at in Chapter 6 on page 90, things like your checking account, savings account, money markets, Treasury bills—basically any assets that you can turn into spending money fairly quickly without a loss.

Investments. Investment assets include stocks, mutual funds, and annuities. (See Chapter 6 for a refresher on what these are.) These are assets you hold in accounts you designate to fund education, home or car purchases, or other major expenses you anticipate and prepare for, as well as your retirement assets. Since this category includes retirement assets, you'll list your retirement accounts such as IRAs, as well as any retirement plans (from current and previous employers), such as 401(k)s and 403(b)s.

Coming up with a value for a pension plan can be a little tricky. If it has a lump-sum value, then list it. If it lists a monthly pension amount you'd receive if you retired today, you can multiply that monthly payment amount by 240 (the amount you'd receive over twenty years). This should approximate the lump sum value.

Property. Your property includes assets that you own, that are tangible (something you can touch), but that don't fit into the other asset categories. Your home is an example of property, as is any other real estate you own, as well as your car, furniture, jewelry, electronic equipment, and so on.

Liabilities (What you owe)

The liabilities section of your net worth statement is, quite simply, a list of how much you owe. If you owe $10,000 on your car, then that is a $10,000 liability. It's not the amount of your payment, but the total amount you owe.

Your liabilities might include credit card balances, car loans, consumer loans, student loans, home loans, or loans from your parents.

Now it's your turn.

On the next page you'll find a sample net worth statement you can use to generate a statement of your own. It includes all the categories we've discussed, so you can use it as a worksheet now and in the years to come. Feel free to make a stack of photocopies—if you keep them handy you'll be more likely to use them to check your progress on a regular basis.

Net Worth Statement as of (date)_____		
Assets		
Cash		
	Checking accounts	
	Savings accounts	
	CDs (certificates of deposit)	
	Life insurance (cash surrender value)	
	Treasury bills	
	Other cash	
Total Cash		
Investments (non-retirement accounts)		
	Stocks	
	Bonds	
	Mutual funds	
	Annuities	
	Other investments	
Investments (retirement accounts)		
	IRAs, 401(k), pension, other	
Total Investments		
Property		
	Home (market value)	
	Real estate (market value)	
	Automobile (current value)	
	Other property	
Total Property		
Total Assets (Cash + Investments + Property)		
Liabilities		
	Credit card debt	
	Car loan	
	Consumer loans or installments	
	Student loans	
	Home and real estate loans	
	Life insurance loans	
	Other liabilities	
Total Liabilities (add above liabilities)		
Net Worth (Total Assets – Total Liabilities)		

ARE YOU ON SCHEDULE?

Are you on track to becoming More than a Millionaire by the time you retire? Where should you be at this stage in your life as an investor?

The answers to those questions depend on your income, your age, your ability to save, and a host of other factors. Out of hundreds of asset classes, ratios, and other indicators of how you're doing, we're going to focus on two key items: your retirement account and your debt load. If you take care of those, the rest will follow. If you work steadily to build your retirement account, and just as steadily to eliminate your debt, you'll reach your goal of being financially secure when you retire.

First let's look at your retirement accounts. If you're on the More than a Millionaire plan, the following table offers some guidance about where you should be today, so your retirement accounts will have $1 million in them in the 35th year of the plan. There are more than a million variations on the parameters we can use to anticipate your income, your investment earnings, and so on. But for our purposes here I've chosen guidelines that are probably similar to your circumstances, give or take...you can adjust them as needed.

Let's assume that on day one of your plan you make $30,000 a year and begin investing 5% of your gross income every month. You average 3% annually in pay raises, and put half of your raises into investments. We'll assume your investments earn a conservative 6%

return on average over the course of the 35 years. You allocate your savings across various types of accounts as follows:

1. First you put all you can into your retirement plan pre-tax. Generally you can do this all the way up to 15% of your income.

2. You put additional dollars into a Roth IRA up to the allowable amount.[39]

3. Additional savings go into an after-tax and taxable account.

Retirement Accounts	
	Total amount you should have in your retirement accounts
Start	0
End of Year 5	$16,637
Year 10	$54,293
Year 15	$122,722
Year 20	$235,470
Year 25	$411,252
Year 30	$675,834
Year 35	More than a Million: $1,064,571
(If your investment earnings average 8.75% instead of 6%, then you hit the More than a Million mark at the end of year 30 and retire 5 years earlier.)	

[39] There are limitations to how much you can put into a Roth IRA in a single year. As of this writing, if you are 50 years of age or older the allowable amount is $6,500 a year.

Now let's take a look at your debt load. Besides having $1 million in your retirement account, we also want you to be debt free by the time you retire, so I've suggested some guidelines for how much debt you should be carrying relative to the value of your assets as you move closer to your goal. We call it your "debt to assets ratio." To see how your progress compares to numbers I've provided, just take your total debts, or liabilities (from your net worth statement), and divide that number by your total assets (also from your net worth statement).

Debt to Assets Ratio	
	Your total liabilities divided by your total assets should be this number or lower (the lower the better)
Start	Infinity
End of Year 1	100
Year 5	1.6
Year 10	.8
Year 15	.4
Year 20	.2
Year 25	.1
Year 30	.05
Year 35	0
The combination of having a Debt to Assets Ratio of 0 and $1 million in your retirement accounts means you've become More than a Millionaire.	

ANALYZING YOUR NET WORTH STATEMENT

Now that you have your net worth statement, there are a variety of ways to make it work for you. In the financial world we look at how a particular number on the statement compares to another—it's a quick and easy way to assess how you're doing. These comparisons are called "financial ratios," and they're a lot like the ones we looked at in Chapter 5. (See "Analyzing Your Spending Plan" on page 83.) The debt to assets ratio in the table on page 159 is one way of analyzing your net worth statement.

There are hundreds of other ratios you can use to analyze your progress using information from your net worth statement, and hundreds more that use a combination of information from your net worth statement and your spending plan. I've boiled all of those down to three more that, in addition to your debt to assets ratio, are most important to you at this point in your life. Here they are:

- Solvency ratio
- Cash reserves ratio
- Debt to income ratio

Solvency ratio

I'm not sure who came up with this name (probably a banker), but your solvency ratio is the number you get when you divide your total assets by your total liabilities. That number should, at all times, be greater than 1—and the bigger the better.

Remember the first net worth statement I drew up for myself? I don't recall the exact numbers, but the solvency ratio from that statement probably looked something like this:

$$\$28,000 \div \$32,000 = 0.875$$

No, the number was not greater than 1. I had to work very hard, in the beginning, just to get it higher than 1. It just goes to show you that it doesn't matter where you're starting from. What matters most is that you start.

Cash reserve ratio

This is a combination of information from your spending plan and your net worth statement. The cash reserve ratio answers this question: If you didn't have any income coming in, how long could you get by with the cash you have on hand? The general rule of thumb is that you want three to six months of your monthly expenses in cash reserves. Remember, cash is any asset you can quickly convert to actual dollars without incurring heavy fees, and without the risk that its value has fluctuated downward when you need to convert it. Examples of cash accounts include your checking account, savings account, money market funds, short-term CDs, and T-bills.

Amount of Cash ÷ Monthly Expenses = Cash Reserve Ratio

For example, if you have $10,000 in cash for emergency purposes and you spend $2000 a month, then your cash reserve ratio is 5 months.

$$\$10,000 \div \$2,000 \ per \ month = 5 \ months$$

Your goal is to have between 3 and 6 months of cash reserves. If you have more than a 6-month reserve, you'll want to put the excess into an investment that can provide more growth or income than you'll get from most cash accounts.

Debt to income ratio

This is another combination ratio using the net worth statement and spending plan. To find your debt to income ratio, add up all of your liabilities (what you owe) and divide that total by your gross annual income. For example, if you have a gross income of $100,000 a year (it makes my math easy), a mortgage of $150,000, and a car loan of $25,000, then you have a debt ratio of 1.75.

$$(\$150,000 + \$25,000) \div \$100,000 = 1.75$$

Eventually you want to be debt free, but it does take time for most people. Here are some "upper end" guidelines, depending on your age:

Your Age	30	35	40	45	50	55	60
Debt to income ratio	1.8	1.5	1.2	0.85	0.5	0.2	0.0

Once you know how to create a net worth statement and become familiar with how to use it, you'll be able to see exactly where you are on the path to becoming More than a Millionaire. You'll also have some valuable tools to help you gauge your financial health. All of this will make the going easier for you, especially at times when it feels like you're not making progress. I kept my first net worth statement for many years just to keep me motivated...to see how far I'd come when it felt like I was standing still. Keeping it made a difference for me, and it will for you as well.

Get started!

CHAPTER 12

SETTING GOALS—AND ACHIEVING THEM

You've taken stock of your financial health with a net worth statement, and have a plan in place to monitor your progress as you reduce your debt and build your retirement fund by investing a portion of every paycheck. But unless you have specific goals for where your efforts will take you, it's a little like setting out on a long hike with no clue where you're headed. You might enjoy the trip quite a lot, but you're likely to get distracted by interesting side trips (or spending sprees) along the way. Even if you manage to stay on the main path, who knows where you'll end up? And how will you know when you get there?

It might be fine to let spontaneity rule the day when you head out for a leisurely walk in the woods. But do you think it's wise to be that cavalier about your financial future?

I didn't think so.

Yet that's exactly how many people approach their finances. They seem to believe that as long as they're investing on a regular basis they'll somehow hit their target—only they have no idea what that target is.

Let me explain it another way.

Kevin Durant, I think it's safe to say, is a pretty good basketball player. He was an NBA All-Star five years running, and in 2014 was named the league's Most Valuable Player. He is a great free throw shooter, averaging over 88%.

I am a great teacher, and with only a couple of hours of instruction I can teach you how to win a free-throw contest against Kevin Durant—provided...of course...that we blindfold Kevin Durant, spin him around a few times, and put sound-cancelling headphones on him.

Now, you might say that's ridiculous. How can Kevin Durant hit a free throw he can't see and has no way to locate? Good question. Here's one for you: How can you hit a financial goal you haven't identified and can't possibly see?

Whether you're shooting hoops or planning for your retirement, knowing what your goals are is essential if you're to have a fighting chance of attaining them. You need long-term goals to make sure you have a clear trajectory so you'll know how to map your route from here to there. You also need intermediate goals to help you pace yourself, so you can spread your efforts out across the 30 or 40 years between now and retirement. That way you won't find yourself facing an impossible uphill climb when you expected to be in the home stretch. As an added bonus, when you also set short-term goals you'll be able to celebrate each time you reach one of them. The end result will feel much more attainable, and the whole process will certainly be more enjoyable.

Then why is it that so many people skip this part of planning their financial futures? I'd say it's for the same reason they wait too long to start investing in the first place. There's always a reason to wait, no matter how old you are, or how much—or how little—time you have before you want to retire. It's just too easy to put it off until...well, that's the point. Until, until, until...too often until it's too late.

Don't let this be the story of your life:

Age 21-30: I can't invest now. "There's plenty of time. I'm young and don't make a lot of money yet. I'll wait until I start making more, then I'll start investing."

Age 30-45: I can't invest now. "It takes every dollar I make to take care of my growing family. Between them and my house payment, there's just nothing left over for investing. When the kids are older, expenses will be lower. Then I'll start saving for my retirement."

Age 45-55: I can't invest now. "My kids are in college. It's all I can do to manage to pay their tuition and housing expenses. I'll wait until they get out of college, then I'll really get serious about investing."

Age 55-65: I can't invest now. "I know I should, but things aren't breaking for me in my career like they were when I was younger. It's difficult for a person my age to find a better-paying job. I guess I'll ride along and see what happens and hope for the best."

Age 65 and beyond: I wish I had started sooner.

Sadly, that's a pretty accurate account of the financial life story for far too many people. According to the Pensions Rights Center, in 2015, for households (that means two or more people) that included at least one person who was at least 65 or older, the median income was $38,515. That means half of all those households were getting by on *less than* $38,515. For individuals 65 years or older, the median income was $22,887.[40] In 2016, the average benefit from Social Security for an individual retired worker (not necessarily 65 years old) was $1,348 a month or about $16,000 a year.[41] So, for most people, and certainly for a household where both were taking Social Security retirement benefits, those monthly checks from the government provided the majority of their retirement income.

Counting on Social Security to fund your retirement is not, I would suggest, the best of long-term plans. Even if you're willing to spend your golden years living on $16,000 a year, more or less, the truth is you may not even be able to count on that. You've probably heard that Social Security is facing some tough times ahead, as the proportion of people taking benefits will increase relative to the number of young people paying into the fund. Clearly there will have to be some changes in the next 30 years if the fund is to remain solvent, and there's no way of knowing what those changes will be. It just makes sense for you to strive to be financially independent

---

[40] Pension Rights Center, "Income of Today's Older Adults," http://www.pensionrights.org/publications/statistic/income-today's-older-adults, accessed January 5, 2017.

[41] Social Security Administration [US], "Fact Sheet: Social Security," https://www.ssa.gov/news/press/basicfact.html, accessed January 5, 2017.

without counting on what was once considered the Social Security "safety net."

Assuming you agree with me, translating that desire for financial independence into action is easier said than done, and it's where a lot of people fall short. It's been my experience that, of all the people I talk to about financial planning and about how to secure their retirement income, about 5% actually succeed. That's right, 5%. One in twenty. When I give educational seminars and share this fact, I scan the audience, usually about 40 people, and say, "So, the probabilities are that two of you will become financially independent." I look around the room, shake my head, smile, and say, "A whole bunch of you right now are wondering who that other person is." This always generates a chuckle. Everyone thinks they will get there. But thinking it is one thing. Doing it is another.

BE SMART ABOUT YOUR RETIREMENT

So how can you beat the odds? What does it take to make sure you'll be in that elite 5% of people who actually retire with the kind of financial freedom you're dreaming of right now?

The answer takes us back to where we started: You set goals. I've found that to be the one critical step taken by the people who actually get there, and it seems to make all the difference. To be precise, successful people set SMART goals—that is, they use a tool based on five key principles that will help you reach the goals you set for any area of your life.

How does it work? Just apply these simple principles to your goal-setting:

S	Specific targets
M	Measurable action
A	Ardent desire
R	Realistic objectives
T	Time frame

There's one more thing, and it may be the most important principle of all: *Your goals must be in writing.*

Then take it one step further and tell a helpful and encouraging friend. Accountability is a powerful motivator.

Now let's look at each of these principles as they pertain to your finances.

Specific targets. It's not good enough to say, "I want to be financially independent one day." What does that mean? How much money will make you "financially independent"? You must define it. This book is designed to help you become More than a Millionaire—someone with a rich and rewarding life that includes $1 million or more in a retirement fund. With that goal in mind, you could set for yourself the specific target to have $1 million in your retirement fund. You might choose to modify your target to be more or less than that. Just be sure you define it as a specific number.

You'll also want to set some intermediate targets, so you have something to shoot for (so to speak...Kevin Durant and his blindfold notwithstanding) at various intervals along the way. The information on page 184, "The Rule of 72," will help you gauge how fast you can expect your money to grow. Building your fund to 1 million dollars may feel a bit daunting, but as you reach each of your shorter term goals you'll feel a sense of accomplishment that will inspire you to keep going. You know what they say…by the mile it's a trial, by the inch a cinch.

Measurable action. Your stated goals need to describe measurable action. What will you do to reach your specific targets? How much do you need to save, perhaps on a monthly basis, measured in dollars? That's the measure you will use to assess whether you're doing what you need to do to reach your goals. Then, when you take stock of your progress, you can easily see why you're on track, reaching the targets you've set—or why you're not:

- Did you take action? Either you did it or you didn't.
- Did you take action but still didn't reach your target? You can adjust your measurable action to make sure you reach your next target.

That's a whole lot better than finding out on your sixtieth birthday that you weren't putting enough away to fund the retirement you've been dreaming of.

Ardent desire. My son had a 3.5 grade point average going for him one semester in high school. I said to him, "Wouldn't it be great if you had a 4.0?"

He said, "Yeah, Dad, that would be great. But I don't want it that much."

You've got to want to attain your goals. They must represent something important to you, because if they don't, you won't be sufficiently motivated to stick with your plan. Life will happen and knock you off the trail.

If you find yourself wavering or wandering, and having trouble sticking to your plan of action, set aside some time to take stock of why you planned to do it in the first place.

- Do you want to work until your dying day?
- What if you're unable to work when you begin to age?
- Even if you love your work—and especially if you don't— would it be nice to have the option to retire at age 60 or 65, or at least by age seventy?
- In an ideal scenario, how would you like to spend your days in your senior years?
- What will your life be like when you're seventy or eighty years old if you become More than a Millionaire?
- What will it be like if you don't?

Realistic objectives. Now, I have to be careful on this one. Back in the mid-1980s when I first started talking to clients and teaching seminars, I used to say, "You must be realistic. For example, I am 5'9" tall. I am not going to win the NBA slam-dunk championship." I stopped using that example when a seminar attendee informed me that Spud Webb, a towering figure at 5'7", had won the slam-dunk championship in 1986.

Sometimes we make assumptions about limitations on what we're capable of. If we allow those assumptions to hang around in the back of our minds long enough, we begin to behave as though they're true...and ultimately they *become* true. Certainly we can't do everything, but be careful of putting up walls where none exist.

At the same time, make sure your goals aren't so big that it costs you way too much to reach them. Becoming a multi-millionaire isn't worth it if you have to become a stranger to your kids in the process.

Take stock of what you'd like to achieve. Go for your dream, but don't throw realism out the window.

Time frame. Set specific time frames for when you will achieve your long-term goal as well as your intermediate goals. Putting a target out there in hopes it will happen "someday" won't have much power to move you forward today.

How long do you want your child to be in the fourth grade? One year, right? (Yes, there's a reason they make those desks so small: so they won't fit an 18-year-old.) And what happens if a child starts falling behind? You get her the help she needs and encourage her to work harder, right? But if you don't set a time frame for her progress, you won't even know she's fallen behind.

Of course, the time frame for your long-term financial goals will probably be much longer than a year, but it's just as important. Set yourself a 35-year goal for retirement, or 25 or 40 years, or whatever you choose. For your intermediate goals, you might set a target for the amount you want to have in your retirement account at the end of each year, or at five- or ten-year markers.

Write it down.

Most important of all, you must put your SMART goals in writing. Putting it all down on paper and reviewing it on an ongoing basis has a powerful psychological impact. For one thing, it transforms the goals and the steps you'll take to achieve them from an idea in your head into something that exists in the real world...and that's powerful.

Also, there's a relationship between the act of writing and the subconscious mind, and researchers are just beginning to understand it. According to Dr. Virginia Berninger, a professor of educational psychology at the University of Washington, when you use your hand to physically write something on a piece of paper, it engages both hemispheres of your brain, including huge areas that are involved in thinking and memory as well as storing and managing information.[42] It also activates parts of the brain in which you create new ideas,[43] which, I would argue, might help you find creative ways to achieve your goals.

---

[42] Gwendolyn Bonds, "How Handwriting Trains the Brain: Forming Letters Is Key to Learning, Memory, Ideas," *The Wall Street Journal*, October 5, 2010. http://www.wsj.com/articles/SB10001424052748704631504575531932754922518, accessed June 21, 2016.

[43] Maria Konnikova, "What's Lost as Handwriting Fades," *The New York Times*, http://www.nytimes.com/2014/06/03/science/whats-lost-as-handwriting-fades.html, accessed June 21, 2016.

Even if you can't tear yourself away from your computer keyboard, typing your goals and saving them where you can review them on a regular basis will dramatically increase the likelihood you'll achieve them. Print out those specific targets and post them on a wall where you'll see them every day. Or turn them into wallpaper for your tablet or smart phone, so you can't help but see them many times throughout the day. The more you keep your long-term and intermediate goals in your thoughts, the more you'll modify the little things you do each day to help you reach them.

Tell a friend.

Let's face it, we are social creatures. We thrive in close association with other humans. We also reach our goals more easily when another human is involved. If you enlist a friend to be an accountability partner in your journey to financial freedom, he or she will help keep you honest by reviewing your progress. There's a reason the buddy system has been around for a very long time.

It probably goes without saying—but I'll say it anyway—that there's no benefit in choosing Debbie Downer as your buddy, or someone who would rather blow his last dollars on a weekend getaway than put them into a retirement fund. Your ally needs to be someone who understands, as you do, the value of creating SMART goals and of doing the little things you need to do each day to realize them. He or she should be the kind of person who can help you stay on track, without making you feel like a first-class loser if you falter now and then. Choose someone who will offer encouragement and support, as well as accountability, and who will be glad to have you offer the same in return.

Does it work? Research by Dr. Gail Matthews[44] found that those who checked in with a partner on a regular basis had a 76% chance of accomplishing their goals, while those who simply thought about their goals succeeded just 43% of the time. Dr. Matthews followed her subjects for just four weeks, but their success in that short period of time is a real testament to just how powerful this tactic is.

You may wander off the path if you're out there on your own, but if you've made a commitment to someone you respect, I promise you'll be far more likely to stay the course.

DEFINE YOUR GOALS—ALL OF THEM

Of course, the first step in any goal setting process is knowing what you're aiming for. What do you want to achieve? You're reading a book called *More than a Millionaire*, so I think I can safely assume that having a nice bundle of money in your account is on the list. But is that all?

Since this is a book about financial goals, most of our discussion so far has been about accumulating $1 million. However, as I mentioned way back in Chapter 1, "Which Mountains Do You Want to Climb?" one of my goals in writing this book is to inspire you to achieve much more than that. With wealth comes responsibility and

---

[44] Dominican University of California, "Study Focuses on Strategies for Achieving Goals, Resolutions," http://www.dominican.edu/dominicannews/study-highlights-strategies-for-achieving-goals, accessed January 5, 2017.

opportunity, and I encourage you to embrace both of those with great passion. Let me explain.

Remember the story of the Good Samaritan? One day as he was traveling, he happened upon a man who had been beaten, stripped, robbed, and left for dead. Two other people had already passed him by, unwilling to help. But the Samaritan stopped and cleaned the man's wounds with oil and wine, hoisted him onto the Samaritan's own donkey, and took him to an inn where he cared for the beaten and battered man overnight. Before leaving the next morning, the Samaritan paid the innkeeper two dinarrii, saying, "Whatever you spend beyond that, I will repay you when I return."[45]

Now, we've all heard this story plenty of times, and most people remember it as a reminder to help those in need. But there's another angle on it that few people notice. As compassionate as the Samaritan was, he probably wouldn't have been able to help—or certainly not to the degree he did—if all he had was a compassionate heart. He had money as well. Oil and wine were very expensive in those days, and a poor man wouldn't have been traveling with a donkey. If the Samaritan hadn't been wealthy, he might have had to leave the unfortunate soul by the side of road with nothing more than a kind word. And he certainly couldn't have left the innkeeper with a virtual blank check to care for the injured fellow.

There are lots of reasons to become wealthy, as you know well enough. But to me, one of the most important reasons is that it vastly expands your ability to do good in the world. Money doesn't fix

---

[45] Luke 10:30–37, World English Bible, http://ebible.org/web/LUK10.htm, accessed June 28, 2016.

everything, but it can make lots of things much, much easier. It also opens doors—yes, it opens doors to fancy restaurants and high-end resorts, but it also helps you gain access to influential people and to opportunities to have a positive impact on your community, or even on a global scale. Heck, in more simple terms it just makes it easier to lend a helping hand to a friend or neighbor. And on an even more personal level it allows you to buy experiences you'll treasure, and that will create cherished memories for your family.

I believe attaining financial wealth is a worthy goal for most anyone—not for the money alone, but primarily for what you become because of it. Just as money compounds over time, so will your influence and ability to help others. When you work at defining your goals and begin to watch your money grow, be careful not to lose sight of those things that are more important. Agreed? I ask you trust me on this: You can be a millionaire *and* have a significant life helping others. In my opinion, based on my 30-plus years of experience as a financial advisor, it is much easier to be a millionaire *and also happy* (you do want both, yes?) if, along the way, you help others who are less fortunate than you.

So in strictly financial terms, the goal is to have $1 million in your retirement and investment accounts. But realizing the goal of becoming More than a Millionaire means also setting targets to help others, embrace your responsibility to your fellow earthlings, and make a positive difference in the world.

Now let's take a closer look at your financial goals....

Why financial goals are different

There are many kinds of things you might want to accumulate over time. Maybe you love growing your music collection, or enjoy building out that home theater system (the one you *didn't* put on your credit card...right?). Or maybe you get a kick out of adding to your wall of Hoka running shoes. (Full disclosure: I have six pairs...they're really great!)

Building wealth is different from any of those, and from most every other type of acquisition, because of the effect of compounding returns. Let's say you like to collect figurines, and your intermediate goal is to collect three a year. If you meet your specific targets, in ten years you'll have 30 figurines. Pretty simple, yes? But when it's money you're collecting, everything changes. It is more like raising rabbits. You can start out with two, who then produce offspring, and then their offspring give you offspring, who give you lots more offspring...and on it goes. What's even better, unlike the rabbits, money doesn't have a life expectancy. Your first dollars never die— but they do produce offspring, in a manner of speaking, which produces even more offspring. Lots and lots of offspring.

When you invest your dollars you have an opportunity to get a return on your investment in the form of interest, dividends, or increased share value. Then the dollars you gain in that return go on to earn a return, and so on, again and again for years. Just like the bunnies, your earnings are compounded, so your earnings earn money, which earns more money after that. Your money actually does a lot of the work for you. Of course, none of this happens unless you start investing. But with a little discipline, the right plan, a reasonable return, and enough time to allow the magic of compounding to do its thing, you are much more likely to achieve your goals more easily and quickly than if your goal is to have a small hangar full of model airplanes.

Here's an interesting example of the difference.

Imagine a chess board, with the standard 64 squares. If you placed a single grain of wheat on all 64 squares, and then picked them up, you would have 64 grains of wheat. Simple enough. But there's a great story that demonstrates what would happen if you could somehow apply the power of compounding to those grains of wheat. I know, it seems like a stretch, but...stay with me on this.

As the story goes, the supposed inventor of chess, an ancient Indian minister named Sessa, pleased his king with his invention. The king asked him what he would like in return for this great game. Sessa said he simply wanted one grain of wheat for the first square on the chessboard, two grains for the second square, four for the third and eight for the fourth, and so on, doubling the number of grains sequentially for each of the 64 squares on the chess board. The critical element here is that he asked that the number of grains double for each consecutive square.

The king, reportedly, laughed at the meager prize for such a brilliant invention. He stopped laughing when the court treasurers reported that the "meager prize" amounted to the kingdom's entire resources of wheat—18,446,744,073,709,551,615 grains, to be exact (but who's counting?).[46] Depending on who's telling the story, Sessa

---

[46] Malba Tahan, *The Man Who Counted: A Collection of Mathematical Adventures*, New York: W.W. Norton & Co., 1993, pp. 110–115.

was either given the wheat or executed. We can only hope his wisdom was duly rewarded.

Now, sorry to say, the return on your investment won't double every year (check out the Rule of 72 on page 184 to find out how long that would actually take), and you don't have 64 years to reach your goal. Then again, you don't need 18 quintillion dollars to fund a happy retirement. Silliness aside, the point here is to show you the very real power of compounding.

Why is it so important at this stage of your life as an investor? At first glance, it may seem that its benefits are something you can look forward to, but they won't really help you much until they've had time to materialize...maybe 20 or 30 years from now when you can sit back and enjoy seeing that wonderful, seven-figure balance in your account.

But that's only part of the picture. Compounding also plays a key role in your goal setting right now, starting today. Remember our discussion of SMART goals? Measurable Action is the second step in that process (see page 171): You need to decide what you will do to achieve your specific targets. In this case, how much money will you need to set aside each month to make sure you reach those targets? Do you just divide $1 million by the number of months until you retire? Of course not...thank goodness. (If that were the case, even if you had 40 years to reach your goal, or 480 months, you'd have to save $20,833. Every month.) The power of compounding starts working for you the day you make your first investment, because it allows you to create a realistic plan that makes sense.

How Much Do You Need to Save?

If you want to have $1 million by the time you're 60 years old, will saving $50 each month get you there? Will $100? Or do you need to save $1,000 a month, or more? How in the world are you supposed to know?

The answer depends on four variables:

1. The amount of money you have now
2. The amount of money you've set as the specific target for your end goal
3. The amount of time you have to reach your goal
4. The return on your investment

That's it. Just four. Easy to get a handle on it, right? The best part is that you have some degree of control over all four variables.

For the first three, either you already know the answer, or you pretty much get to call the shots. The amount of money you have to start with is probably a given, more or less. And if you haven't already decided how much you want to end up with, it's up to you. Maybe that's $1 million, or maybe it's something else. Whatever your target number is, it may seem like a long way from here to there. But even if you start at zero, if you're disciplined about adding money into the account on a regular basis, you'll reach your goals. How can I be so sure?

Because of that third variable: time. First of all, you get to decide how long you're willing to wait to reach your goal. Are you determined to retire in 20 years? Or do you love your work so much you plan to keep at it as long as you can, so you don't expect to need that retirement fund for maybe 40 or 50 years. Either way, time is the key element that allows compounding to work its magic, like the 64 squares on Sessa's chessboard, which turned a single grain of wheat into a king's ransom. As the years go by your money will generate more money, which will in turn generate still more.

At your age you have time on your side—but the only way it will work in your favor is if you start saving now. It couldn't be simpler: The sooner you start saving, the more time you have to save. Remember (refer back to page 167 at the beginning of this chapter if you don't), the biggest reason people fail financially is that they never start. But that's not going to happen to you, because you *are* going to start now. (If there's still any doubt in your mind, keep reading, and I'll show you how much you can achieve when you let time work for you.)

Out of all of our four variables, you probably have the least amount of control over how much your return on investment will be. Even so, with a smart investment strategy (see Chapter 14, "Your More than a Millionaire Portfolio") you can give yourself an excellent chance to have a return that will take you where you want to go. Of course, there are no guarantees; if someone tries to give you one, run fast in the other direction, because it's just not possible. The reality is that no one knows exactly what kind of return you'll get over the next 20 or 30 or 40 years. But if you're smart and disciplined, and if you educate yourself and plan carefully, your return will take care of itself over the long haul.

So while I can't give you guarantees, I can give you some guidelines that will help you formulate some realistic expectations, which in turn will help you make critical choices about taking measurable actions as part of your SMART goal setting strategy.

The rule of 72

We've noted that your money isn't going to double every year, like the grains of wheat on Sessa's chessboard. But it will double over time. To give you a feel for what compounding your return means to you in real dollars, let's take a look at how much time it actually takes: If you start with $100, and don't add any more money to it, how long will it take for the compounding return to grow that money into $200?

There's something called "the rule of 72" that has been extremely valuable to me as an investor, and I think it will help you as well. It's a little trick that lets you figure out how long it takes that money of yours to double. Now, of course, how long it takes depends entirely on how much of a return you get on that $100. If you're earning an average of 4% a year, obviously it will take much longer than if you can manage to earn an average of 10%.

The rule of 72 takes that into account, and makes it all very simple: 72 divided by the rate of return equals the number of years it will take your money to double. Here are some examples:

How many years will it take to double your money?		
Rate of return	**Rule of 72**	**Number of years**
4%	72 ÷ 4 =	18
6%	72 ÷ 6 =	12
8%	72 ÷ 8 =	9
10%	72 ÷ 10 =	7.2

As you can see, your rate of return makes a dramatic difference, especially when you have time to let your compounding returns work for you.

What's your measurable action?

Unless you have a cool $500,000 sitting around, you can't just wait around for your money to double to get you to your goal of $1 million. You need to know how much to invest on a regular basis so you can realize that goal—even if you're starting out with nothing. To find the answer, we can apply the four variables we talked about on page 182, as follows:

1. **The amount of money you have now.** To make our work easy, let's assume you're starting with zero. If you already have something saved, so much the better. You can use the rule of 72 to get a rough estimate of how much that money will grow in the next 30 or 40 years.

2. **The amount of money you've set as the specific target for your end goal.** You guessed it, I'm all about keeping

things simple, so let's use our stated goal of $1 million. If your target is higher or lower than that, you can make adjustments accordingly.

3. **The amount of time you have to reach your goal.** This is completely dependent on your personal situation, and, assuming you remain healthy enough to work as long as you choose to, it's probably the one variable you have the most control over. For those reasons I've set things up so you can plug in different numbers, explore different options. You can see what it would take to get you permanently out on the golf course in 20 years, if that's what you want—and if you're willing to be disciplined enough to get there. If you'd rather spend more of your money now and don't mind working another 35 or 40 or even 45 years, I'll show you how little it will take to let you reach your goal in that amount of time.

4. **The return on your investment.** Ahh, this is where it gets interesting, and where you should also consider a few different scenarios. I believe it's reasonable to aim for an average annual return of 10%. Why? Well, the average annual rate of return on the U.S. stock market (not including any international stocks) from 1926 (just before the great depression) to 2009 (just after the great recession) was about 10%. As you can imagine, in some years the rate of return was better than 10%, and in others it was worse. It's possible to improve your chances of getting a better return (see my suggestions for a sample portfolio in Chapter 14),

but for our purposes here, let's stick to the middle ground. When you do your own goal setting you may want to use a lower rate of return, just to play it safe. But I would never recommend assuming you'll earn more.

Now that we have our variables worked out, let's run some numbers. As a starting point, let's assume:

1. you're starting with nothing,
2. you'd like to stop working in 35 years,
3. your goal is to have $1 million when you retire, and
4. you'll earn a 10% average annual return.[47]

For your measurable action you'll need to set aside $262 a month.

What if we change the variables a bit? What if you have just 30 years to invest instead of 35? With all the above other assumptions, you will need to set aside $439 a month. Yes, dropping five years off your time frame makes that much difference. It's because of the compounding effect. A snowball rolling downhill gets most of its mass during the last part of the trip. It's the same for investing.

How about 25 years? Applying the above assumptions again, it would take $748 a month. Now do you see why I've been harping on the importance of starting now?

What about different rates of return? Let's say you have 35 years to reach your goal, but your portfolio only earns 8% instead of

---

[47] 1/12 of 10% per month.

10%. How much do you need to invest to end up with $1 million, if you start with nothing? $434 a month. Remember, with a 10% return you only needed to invest $262. That's right, just a 2% difference in return makes that much of a difference. If you earn 6% instead of 10%, you'll need to save $699 each month. Another big jump.

As you can see, reaching your goal is all about finding the right combination of time and return.

What if you're the cautious, conservative type. You've heard the stock market is risky business, and don't want to take chances with your retirement fund, so you'd rather put all your money into CDs. They're safe. They're insured by the federal government.[48] And you know up front exactly how much interest they'll earn. How will that work out for you once we apply our four variables?

As of this writing, certificates of deposit are paying around 1%. Not much...but let's see how it plays out. Just for fun, how much do you think you would need to invest, on a monthly basis, if you put all of it into CDs paying a 1% return? $1,988 a month. And if you had only 25 years to do so, instead of 35, then you'd "only" need to up it to $2,933 a month. Do those CDs still look like a good idea?

Enough speculating about what choices I think you might make. I've prepared a chart for you that lets you plug in a variety of numbers based on the variables that might actually make sense in your life. Play with it a bit, so you can get a sense of what your options are. This is real-world, by-the-numbers stuff, so you can have

---

[48] Bank Certificates of Deposits are almost always FDIC insured.

hard numbers to use as you make these critical decisions. This is no time for guesswork. It's just too important.

How much do you need to invest each month to reach your goal of $1 million when you retire?					
		Your expected rate of return			
		4%	**6%**	**8%**	**10%**
Years until you retire	**45**	661	362	189	95
	40	844	500	285	157
	35	$1,091	$699	$434	$262
	30	$1,437	$991	$667	$439
	25	$1,939	$1,436	$1,045	$748
	20	$2,718	$2,153	$1,687	$1,306

If you want to play with the numbers even more, there's a great website that will let you do that. Go to www.Calculator.net, then click on "Financial Calculators" on the top left side of screen, and click on "Retirement Calculator" right under the "Retirement" heading.[49] The page that pops up has a calculator right in the center, called "How to Save for Your Retirement." It does exactly what we've done here, only it lets you plug in any numbers you wish for the same four variables we've been using. You can even add the amount of money you have on hand now. The calculator will show you how much you'll need to invest each month to reach your goal.

---

[49] Or type in this address: http://www.calculator.net/retirement-calculator.html

YOU HAVE MORE OPTIONS THAN YOU THINK

So far we've been looking at this primarily as a way to figure out how much you need to save to reach your goal. If you're 20 years old and expect to work until you're 65, you can reach your $1 million goal with just a $95 monthly savings plan. Hopefully that's a number you can handle, especially if you invest first and spend what's left. (If it's not, hang in there—I have a solution for that, too...just keep reading.) But what if you're 35 years old and want to retire at 65, so you only have 30 years to reach your goal? Assuming you expect to nail that 10% average annual return, you'll need to save $439 each month. Ouch. That might be more than you can manage.

A different strategy is to figure out what you can afford to set aside, and let that dictate when you'll be able to retire. I'll assume you're still 35 (that last paragraph didn't shock you into the next decade, did it?), but you really can't spare more than about $150 a month. With a 10% return it will take at least 40 years to reach that $1 million mark. Yikes—that means you'll have to work until you're 75 years old. Not what you were hoping for.

Don't get discouraged. There's a third way to approach this. We've been assuming all along that you'll start investing a given amount of money and never change it. But that's not your only option.

What if you could start with a lower amount than the numbers we've been looking at, and then increase your investment as your income increases over the years? What then?

It's not only a workable plan, it's also one that won't cramp your lifestyle today.

"But wait," you say, "my income hasn't increased all that much in the past few years, and I'm strapped for cash every month. I'm not sure I can count on making more money in the future—and even if I do, I'd like to be able to use some of the added income to give myself some breathing space. I can't imagine putting it all toward retirement."

I hear you, and I feel your pain. But if you'll allow me, I can show you some tried and true strategies that will significantly increase your chances of getting more substantial raises, and getting them more often. I'll even show you how you can use that extra cash to give yourself more spending money each month, and at the same time get yourself closer to that $1 million mark more quickly than you could manage with what you're able to save right now.

Turn the page to see how you can make it happen.

CHAPTER 13

 INCREASE YOUR INCOME
FOR A FASTER ROUTE TO BECOMING
MORE THAN A MILLIONAIRE

You've set your goals, and run some numbers to see what it will take to accumulate $1 million by the time you'd like to retire. If the amount of money you'll need to save each month to reach your goal seems like too great a strain on your budget, don't get discouraged. There are a variety of things you can do to increase your cash flow so you can allocate more to your retirement account—and no, you won't need to pinch pennies for the rest of your working life. Let me show you what I mean.

First, let's think about what you can do to increase your income. There are three ways to do that:

- Take on a second job.
- Get a raise—that is, increase the income you receive from the job you have.
- Get a better job that pays more.

Take on a second job

There are obvious limitations to this idea. First, you'll be left with little or no free time, or not enough time with your family or for giving back to your community. Besides, if you deplete your energy by working a bunch of extra hours, it's likely you'll be less effective in your primary job, which makes it unlikely you'll ever really succeed there.

Working a second job might be a necessary band-aid to get you through a crunch time financially, but it's not a good long-term solution. Options 2 and 3, getting a raise or getting a job that pays more, may require a bit more effort. But the results are likely to be far more personally rewarding. They certainly offer greater dividends (financially and otherwise) in the long run. So let's focus on those.

Get a raise

Whether you work for a multinational corporation with a built-in schedule of semi-annual raises, or a local mom-and-pop operation where Mom is the CEO and Dad is the whole HR department, it's to your advantage to be proactive about managing your career in a way that puts your income on an upward trajectory. Don't kid yourself— you have far more control over whether or not your income increases in the years to come than you may realize.

It's really not that complicated. You simply need to make yourself more valuable as an employee. If you do, it follows that you'll be paid more for the extra value you bring to the company you work for. I promise you, people who consistently deliver a stand-out performance get rewarded—maybe not in the time frame they'd like, but eventually they do. And anyway, wouldn't it feel better to attract a raise and know you deserve it than to sit around needing one when you haven't done anything to earn it?

With that in mind, and your More than a Millionaire goals as your incentive, let's get you started on a strategy to that will make reaching those goals far easier than it would be on your current income alone. I've put together a baker's dozen of things you can do, starting today, to make yourself the kind of valuable employee who will attract a raise...and then another raise, and another one after that.

1. **Develop the power habits.** What are those?

   - **Be on time**. A friend of mine says that if you're 15 minutes early, you're on time. If you're on time, you're late. If you're late, that is unacceptable.

   - **Be polite.** Say, "Thank you," and, "You're welcome." Open doors for people. In the simplest interactions you have with other people, let them see that you respect and care about them. Those small gestures will stay with them for a long time.

   - **Be enthusiastic,** even when you don't feel like it. Especially when you don't feel like it. A friend of mine said, "If you act enthusiastic, you'll be enthusiastic." Do I always feel that way? Of course not. But my clients wouldn't know that. And sometimes I fool myself into feeling that way, even on a bad day.

   - **Always ask yourself, "How can I be helpful?"** Then go do it.

If you do nothing more than implement those four habits, you'll be ahead of 95% of your peer group.

2. **Be the go-to person** in your company or your department. Make yourself available for extra projects, even if that means doing some work on your own time. Speak up and ask for opportunities—don't wait for them to fall in your lap. Become the first person your co-workers think of when they need someone they can count on.

3. **Make your boss look good.** This should go without saying, but if there's something you can do to help your boss look like a star, do it. Or if there are things you can say or do to make her job easier, go for it. Take every opportunity to speak highly of her, and keep any negativity to yourself. If you can't find anything positive to say about your boss, find another one.

4. **Take care of you.** Exercise. Don't find the time for it, *make* the time. Eat a healthy diet. Pizza and ramen are easy and tasty, but they won't make you as healthy and energetic as you need to be to perform at your best. When you take care of yourself physically, you will feel better, look better, and have a more productive week.

5. **Do volunteer work.** This will make your life better in so many ways. Find an organization that you sincerely want to help, commit to at least a few hours every month, then show up and be a truly great worker. You'll feel good inside knowing you're supporting a cause that matters to you. You'll also meet

incredible people who share your interests—as well as people who have influence in your community. Win, win, and win.

6. **Enlist the guidance of a mentor** who has already established him- or herself in your field, and who knows what it takes to be successful on your chosen career path. Make sure it's someone you can relate to easily, someone you'd sincerely like to emulate. A good mentor can coach you in ways to excel in the work you do and in making wise choices as you grow professionally.

7. **Read great personal-development books.** Develop a lifetime learning habit that includes reading good books. Make it a point to always have a book going that will help you improve personally or professionally. (Usually it's both.) I've created a three-year reading plan with a list of books to get you started. Look for it in the Appendix, beginning on page 257.

8. **Attend workshops, seminars, and conferences related to your profession.** It doesn't matter what field your job is in. There's a conference or a workshop out there where you can learn how to do it better. If you're in I.T. or medicine or law, the choices are obvious. But even if you're a bagger at a grocery store, you can go to conferences that cater to the grocery or food industries. If you work in the mail room of a corporate office, a time management seminar or a workshop on setting goals will give you a leg up in your next annual review. It will also make you—guess what, a more valuable employee. Be creative. Find something that piques your interest. You'll have fun, meet some interesting people, and get yourself one step closer to that raise.

Some seminars and conferences can be a bit pricy, especially if you need to travel and stay in a hotel to participate. Don't be afraid to ask your supervisor if the company will pick up some or all of the costs. If not, try to find space in your spending plan for it—think of it as an investment in your future.

If that's too much of a stretch right now, there are plenty of workshops and webinars online that you can participate in for as little as $20 or even for free, or in exchange for signing up for the host's newsletter. As with any offering, just make sure it's offered by someone with solid credentials or by an established organization that's related to your field.

9. **Take any course or seminar that helps your communication skills.** A great place to start would be a course in how to write well. You will be communicating all your life, and much of that will be in writing. If you've texted most of your life and think "U B @ crib 2nite?" is a great way to connect, or "This ain't no dozen" is a well-crafted sentence, then you will not go far unless you polish up your skills.

10. **Join Toastmasters.** I did this when I was 27 years old, and it was the single best thing for the lowest cost that I've ever done. In case the idea is new to you, Toastmasters is an international organization that teaches public speaking and leadership skills. There's at least one local group in your community (they're everywhere), and they usually meet every week. You'll learn the technical elements of public speaking, as well as gain the confidence it takes to get up in front of a group and do it well.

You'll also gain experience organizing and leading meetings and events. Overall, you'll pick up exactly the kinds of skills you'll need to become a leader in your profession. Last, but certainly not least, Toastmasters meetings are teeming with community leaders. I can't think of a better place for you to meet people who can help further your career. Check it all out at www.toastmasters.org.

11. **Get credentials in a specialty related to your profession**, by taking specialized courses or sitting for licensing exams or both. Check out the websites for organizations related to your field; most include information about educational opportunities and credentials for professionals. Courses and licensing exams are often offered by community colleges. And of course, most training opportunities are also available online.

12. **Go back to school to get a degree.** Enroll in a community college program, finish that undergrad degree you started a few years back, or get a graduate degree. You can choose to study in any field you like, but it's even better if your major clearly relates to your job. Whatever degree you earn, adding another academic credential to your résumé will demonstrate to your present or future employer that you're serious about self-improvement. You'll also gain knowledge and skills that will help you do your job better.

13. Finally, **if you feel you deserve a raise, ask for it!** Be prepared with a list of ways you've made yourself a valuable employee. If you follow the suggestions in this list, that will be easy to do.

(Whatever you do, do *not* include anything that diminishes the work of others. There's absolutely nothing to be gained by climbing over someone else to get to the top.) Don't bother bringing in a list of the reasons you need the money—your boss and the company you work for are not responsible for your spending plan. Just focus on what you've done for the company, and how you've prepared yourself to take on more responsibilities in the future. Help them see why you're worth what you're asking for.

Get a better job

Every item on my baker's dozen list will help you get ahead in the job you have now, but also wherever you go, in any job you ever have. It will also help you get a new job if that's what you want. That means the job you have today is not necessarily the one you have to stick with.

There are plenty of reasons staying where you are can be a wise choice. Job stability always looks good on a résumé. And if you have a pension plan that's set up to pay you substantially more for every year you stay on the job, it makes sense to take that into account.

But as I've said, being More than a Millionaire is about more than money. If you're not happy with the work you do or the environment you do it in, you won't do yourself any favors by toughing it out indefinitely. And if the prospects of attaining your professional goals look grim if you stay where you are, then it's probably time to think about making a change.

Switching jobs can be an option that serves more than one purpose. If you're currently in a dead-end situation, a fresh start will breathe new energy and enthusiasm into your professional life (with benefits to your personal life as well), even if the work you do in the new job is similar. If you're less than happy in the work you're doing now, let your need for added income be your incentive to make a career switch that takes you closer to doing work you love. You may need to go back to school or enroll in a training program to prepare you for a new job, but don't be afraid to see that as an investment in your future.

Your work should be a reflection of who you are, what you value in life, and the kind of person you want to be. Don't sell yourself short. Strive for the best work experience you can attain. Income is a part of that, to be sure. But it's even more important that you make a commitment to yourself to create a professional life that's just as rewarding personally as it is financially. Life is short; you need to enjoy it—and that includes enjoying your professional life.

What Will You Do with the Extra Cash?

Now that you know how to get yourself a nice raise—this year and next year and every year after that—what will you do with that extra money?

- Take a vacation!
- Buy that entertainment system you considered back in Chapter 4.
- Call your cable company to sign up for HBO and STARZ.

- Revisit your spending plan and adjust the allocations in each category to reflect your increased income.

That last one is more practical than the other ideas. But I have a better one....

- Adjust the allocations in your spending plan to reflect *half* of the increase in your income—and apply the other half directly to your retirement fund.

That's right. You can have your cake and eat it, too...sort of. Use the money from your raise to give yourself some extra breathing room in your spending plan. But before you spread it around to all the categories, put 50% of the increase into the "Investments" category, so it goes right into your retirement account.

I know what you're thinking. You'll feel the impact of your raise a lot more if can use all of it to increase your allotments for food, entertainment, or maybe for rent on a bigger place. That's true—but it's not the whole truth. First, this isn't the last raise you're going to get (because you're still working the baker's dozen tips, right?), so those spending plan allocations are going to keep getting larger as the months and years go by. Second, remember the power of compounding? (If not, refer back to Chapter 12, under "Why Financial Goals Are Different" on page 179.) Every dollar you invest now will grow into more dollars, which will in turn grow into still more dollars, somewhat like the rabbits who have offspring, who then have offspring of their own, and so on. Even if half of your next raise only amounts to a handful of dollars every month, the impact those extra dollars will have on your retirement account is profound.

Here's one example of how powerful that compounding growth can be. Let's take a look at someone who makes $30,000 a year and decides to invest $100 a month...let's call him Ben. Ben does pretty well for himself, and gets some moderate raises every year. He's careful about how he spends his money, but the raises he gets always seem to come along just when he's really bursting the seams on his spending plan, so he uses the money to ease the crunch. Besides, he feels pretty good about that $100 he sets aside every month. He's diligent about sticking to that plan, and does it each and every month for 30 years. To keep things simple, let's say he earns a 10% return each year. At the end of his 30 years, Ben would have about $228,000. Not bad. Ben's pretty proud of himself. And he should be.

Now let's compare Ben's strategy with Jerry's. Jerry also starts off making $30,000 a year, but his investment plan gets off to a slower start. He doesn't read the section in this book where it says, "pay yourself first," so he doesn't put anything into his retirement plan the first year. But then he gets a 4% raise. He goes to his uncle's retirement party and sees first-hand how great it is to retire without financial worries. So Jerry decides to put half of his raise into a retirement fund. That 4% raise means an increase of $1,200 the first year, so Jerry puts $600 into his retirement account that year, or $50 each month. He pats himself on the back. It's a start. The next year Jerry gets another 4% raise, and another 4% raise the year after that, and so on for 30 years. Each year, Jerry applies half of his 4% raise to his retirement account, so the amount he saves each month continues to increase. And like Ben, Jerry also earns a 10% return every year. But 30 years later, when it comes time to retire, Jerry has $1,374,000 in his account. Needless to say, Jerry will be able to buy his grandkids a whole lot more ice cream than Ben can when they come to visit him in his condo on the beach.

So what happened here? Ben saved $100 a month for 30 years, with a return of 10% per year, and ended up with $228,000. Jerry started out saving nothing, but every year he set aside half of his annual 4% raise, earning 10% per year, and after 30 years he had $1,374,000 to retire on.

The point is, the most important thing you can do is start. Start small if you have to, but start. It doesn't take a lot of dollars to make an enormous difference in your ability to reach your More than a Millionaire goals, and in the financial security you can create for yourself over the long term. Even if you start at $0, if you put just half of the money you get in raises into your retirement account, you'll be able to say aloha to the daily grind far sooner—or with a lot more money to enjoy it with. Your choice.

THE FUTURE IS BRIGHTER THAN YOU THINK

Think about what this means regarding what you can accomplish, even if, at this point in your life, you're struggling to set aside as much as you think you need to reach your retirement goals. Remember, at the end of Chapter 12 I promised to show you how to get over the hurdle of feeling unable to set aside a chunk of cash every month for investments. Now you can breathe a little easier, because you have a plan and you know what to do to make it happen.

- You know how to get out of the rut of a stagnant income by making yourself a more valuable employee who deserves—and gets—raises on a consistent basis.

- You know how to decide when it's time to change jobs, if doing so will mean you increase your income as well as get closer to doing the work you love. And after applying my baker's dozen strategies for making yourself a more valuable employee, you'll find many more doors opening for you as you begin your job search.

- And now you know how to use those increases in your income to improve your quality of life today, and also improve your ability to reach your More than a Millionaire goal of financial security.

What's most important is that you start investing now. Today. I'll say it again: How much you save doesn't matter nearly as much as how long you save, so start sooner than later. If you start saving today, the benefits will begin compounding today, and will continue to compound every day, month, and year for the rest of your life.

CHAPTER 14

 YOUR MORE THAN A MILLIONAIRE PORTFOLIO

Once you've made the commitment to make saving a priority, the next step is to make the best possible choices about how you invest that money. Should you play it safe or try to hit it big in the stock market? Is it even possible to hit it big in the stock market, or is that just one huge gamble, sort of like playing the slot machines in Las Vegas? After all, this is your retirement fund we're talking about...your life savings. Wouldn't it make sense to keep that money as safe as possible...maybe put it in the bank where you can earn a nice steady rate of interest with a minimum amount of risk?

I understand your concern about minimizing risk—it just makes sense that you want to avoid taking chances with the money you've worked so hard to earn and save. But keep in mind that you're looking at a long-term investment here; the dollars you save this year are likely to be in that retirement fund for 20, 30, maybe even 40 years. And as we've seen, what looks like a "safe" investment over the next few months might be anything but when you look at the bigger—and longer—view.

Let's take another look at that nice "safe" bank account, or maybe even a CD. It earns you a steady, pre-determined rate of interest, and it's insured by the FDIC so you know you'll never lose your principal (that is, assuming the U.S. government doesn't fail...a reasonable assumption, I'd say). As we discussed in Chapter 6, "The Basic Types of Investments," if you put your money in a savings account or CD for the next 30 or 40 years, the meager amount of interest you'll earn won't begin to make up for the purchasing power those dollars will lose due to inflation. You'll effectively end up with less money than you put in.

A much better plan is to invest your savings in a way that allows it to work for you, so it will eventually generate a comfortable, inflation-proof income. Heck, you worked hard to earn that money in the first place, might as well let it return the favor, right? It only makes sense to turn to the types of investments that will generate a more substantial return. You've been around the block enough times to know that most people put some of their money, if not all of it, in the stock market. But that raises its own set of questions.

- "Is it really possible to get rich investing in stocks?"
- "Isn't playing the stock market a huge gamble?"
- "Isn't there a very real chance I could lose my shirt?"

The answer to each of those questions is, "Yes"—but only if you look at the more extreme examples and exceptions. It is possible to become wealthy investing in stocks, but highly unlikely you'll make a killing in the short run. If you try, you'll be taking a huge gamble, and you'll drastically increase your chances of...losing your shirt. There's no shortage of information out there touting the best way to find the next hot stock, predicting which market trend will peak next, or otherwise suggesting how you can get rich quick. Trust me, there is no such thing as a reliable route to fast-and-easy wealth.

Even if you avoid the crazy get-rich-quick schemes, it is in fact true that investing in the stock market is—in the short run—a gamble, to some degree. After all, stocks do take a tumble from time to time, which means the value of your original investment could fall.

But you can maximize your probability of success if you (a) take a long-term approach to investing, and (b) apply some tried and true strategies that optimize your chance of earning a good return while also minimizing the potential downside.

Sound good? Want to know how?

Smart Strategies for Your Long-Term Investments

Ahh, if only you had a crystal ball—or at least a link to a website that would tell you which stocks are going up and which are about to crash. I know, those websites are out there, or at least there are websites that *claim* to tell you the goods. You can also spend a small fortune on software that promises to give you a green light on the next hot stock, and a big red light on the next big loser.

But here's the thing: Any strategy that promises to make you financially independent by predicting which stocks will go up and which will go down, or by pretending you can stay ahead of the next big trend in the market, is selling little more than a recipe for disaster. The best minds with the most experience in the business can't succeed that way, and they know it. They also know there's a much, much better way.

Smart investors apply three critical strategies as they decide where, when, and how to invest:

- Asset allocation
- Mutual funds
- Dollar cost averaging

We've discussed all of these in some detail in previous chapters, but let's quickly go over them again now that you're ready to start putting them all to work.

Asset allocation

When you allocate your assets across several diverse types of stocks, you create what we call a "balanced stock portfolio." This strategy has been demonstrated again and again over time to be the smartest and best approach. It's not sexy, it doesn't make headlines, and it's not a particularly exciting way to invest—but that's the point. Excitement usually means you're teetering between big rewards and big risks, with all the odds favoring the risks.

Asset allocation is a way to minimize your risk while also giving you an excellent chance you'll see a solid return on your investment over time. As you'll remember, in Chapter 8, "Diversify Your Investments for a Safer and More Profitable Journey," we explored a variety of reasons why allocating your money to a variety of different asset classes (large companies, or "large-cap," vs. small companies, or "small-cap"; growth stocks vs. value stocks; United States companies vs. foreign companies) dramatically increases your earning power, and reduces the amount you'll need to contribute each month to reach your More than a Millionaire goals. Simply put, you allocate your money, or assets, among several diverse types of investments, because when one type of investment goes down (as it most inevitably will at one time or another) another will be going up. The gains in one segment of your portfolio can offset losses in another.

Mutual funds

As we saw on page 116 under "A Better Way to Diversify" in Chapter 8, buying mutual funds instead of individual stocks allows you to reduce your risk even further. Essentially, you pool your money with that of thousands of other individuals like yourself, and buy a small portion of a fund that holds stocks from many different companies. That way, if one of those companies suffers a huge loss or even goes out of business, that loss is diluted by the value of the other companies held by the fund, most of which will presumably be doing better.

Many funds are defined by the types of stocks they hold. One fund may focus on U.S. large-cap value stocks, while another holds only international stocks. Buying shares in several different types of mutual funds is an excellent way to make sure you have a well-diversified, balanced portfolio of stocks.

Dollar cost averaging

You can turn back to Chapter 9, "Dollar Cost Averaging," for a complete explanation of how this works and why it's such a powerful strategy. The short version is that you put a pre-determined (by you, of course) amount of money into your retirement fund every month, regardless of what's happening in the stock market in general or with the investments you hold in your portfolio. That can be hard to do if the market happens to be tanking...you'll feel as though you're throwing good money after bad. But when the value of any given stock is low, you have an opportunity to buy more shares of that stock with your fixed monthly investment. Then, when the market improves and prices go up, the value of all those shares will also go up. That, my friend, is one of the key ways your retirement fund will grow.

But let's be clear: There will indeed be times over the next 30 or 40 years when the market will go down. There are not a lot of absolute guarantees when it comes to investing, but this comes pretty darn close. Be prepared for those downturns, and have a strategy in place ahead of time for how you'll handle them. In all likelihood, the market—that is, your portfolio—will have three negative years in any block of ten years. That's right. *You will lose money three out of every ten years.* Please reread that, underline it, and highlight it. It's just the way the market works, and it's inevitable. I don't know which years are going to see the downturn, and nobody else does, either.

What's critical here is that you stick with your plan, and keep investing every single month, even though it feels like you are throwing your money away. Remember, those years when you're losing money are also the years when you are buying cheap shares. If you're disciplined enough to stick it out, those cheap shares should be your money makers in the long run.

Your Portfolio

Okay, it's time to get down into the dirt and show you how to set up a well-balanced portfolio of stocks. Here's an asset allocation formula that's been tested against past market performance, that makes sense for someone with more than 25 years to invest—someone like you:

- 25% U.S. large-cap value fund
- 25% U.S. large-cap growth fund
- 20% U.S. small-cap value fund
- 20% international developed countries stock fund
- 10% international emerging markets stock fund

This allocation assumes you have access to all the various types of asset classes. That's likely to be true if your money is in an IRA. You can choose from the more than 10,000 mutual funds available, as well as various families of funds. (You can review the details about your options by flipping back to our discussion of mutual funds on page 116 in Chapter 8.) If it feels overwhelming to have to choose the best funds from so many different options, I suggest you start with the family of funds offered by the investment company called Vanguard. They're inexpensive, there's no sales charge, and you can see the asset class of the fund you're buying right there on the company's website. You can find it all at www.Vanguard.com.

If some or all of your money is in a retirement account at work, your choices are likely to be more limited. That is, you may not have access within that account to all the different asset classes. That doesn't mean you shouldn't take full advantage of your company's retirement plan—by all means, you should, especially if the company matches your investment, as many do. If that's the case, don't hesitate to max out the amount they'll match. Hey, it's free money...pretty much a slam-dunk. Even if they don't match your investment, having them take the money out of your paycheck before you get it is a built-in way to literally "pay yourself first." You should be doing that anyway, but if you can eliminate the need for self-discipline—or any lack thereof—from your program, you might as well. Make it easy on yourself.

That said, you'll probably need to make some adjustments to the above portfolio, depending on what kinds of funds are available within your company's plan. Without knowing what's available to you, it's difficult for me to give precise recommendations, so you'll have to use your best judgment to make some logical accommodations. For example, if the company plan has only one international stock fund, combine the 20% allocation for developed countries and the 10% for emerging markets and place 30% of your account into the single international stock fund that's available to you. If the company account doesn't offer a small-cap value fund, look for a small-cap growth or a mid-cap fund to replace it. You won't have the optimum balance of allocations, as I see it, but you can only do the best you can with what you have to work with. The benefits of participating in that company retirement fund outweigh the limitations.

What about bonds?

Back in Chapter 6, "The Basic Types of Investments," we discussed three ways to invest your money: cash, stocks, and bonds. And yet, the portfolio I'm suggesting here has all your money in stocks—a balanced stock portfolio, but 100% stocks nonetheless.

Why put everything into one type of investment?

Well, we've already established that the interest you'll earn on cash investments is so small that you'll effectively lose value on that money over the long term. Cash investments like CDs and money market accounts are the right way to go for your cash reserve account, the money you set aside for unexpected expenses or loss of income, when you need quick access to your money. But you'll only put an amount equivalent to three to six months of income in those accounts. Everything else needs to be in accounts that will earn you a better return.

What about bonds? It's true that a high-quality bond carries less risk than virtually any single stock investment. And while the yield doesn't compare with the average return on a diversified, long-term investment in stocks, it's likely to be higher than most cash investments. So at first glance it might seem like putting some money into bonds would be a good way to balance the volatility of your stock portfolio.

And I would agree with that logic—if you were close to retirement, or if you'd already retired. At that stage in your life, when you'll have fewer years to be investing your money, you'll want to minimize your risk by including the greater stability of bonds in your portfolio. But when you have 25 or 30 or more years to invest, as you do, you have plenty of time to ride out the ups and downs of the stock market, so there's every reason to take full advantage of the higher expected returns of long-term investment in a well-diversified stock portfolio.

Just understand that a portfolio with 100% in stocks will fluctuate in value, so you'll need to remember that it's the growth of your money over time that counts. You should also plan to move a significant amount of that money into bonds as you near retirement age.

REBALANCING

Once you have a well-balanced stock portfolio set up, you're good to go, right?

Right...but not indefinitely. Remember, your portfolio is a vast collection of stocks that fluctuate in value every day. Some go up and some, as we know, go down. And remember, too, that the reason you diversify your portfolio in the first place is that when one asset class goes down, another is likely to go up. So, think about it: You set up your portfolio with 20% of funds in a U.S. small-cap value fund, and 20% in an international developed countries fund (along with the other asset classes I suggested above). Suppose in the first six months the small-cap value fund does well, but the developed countries fund goes down. You might find yourself with 28% of your money in the small-cap value fund, and the developed countries fund is down to 12% of your portfolio. (I've oversimplified matters quite a bit here, but let's go with these numbers as an illustration.) Suddenly your portfolio is no longer in the proper balance. What's a smart investor to do?

You rebalance. In other words, you take money out of the small-cap value fund and put it into the developed countries fund, so they're both back at 20% of the total portfolio.

"But wait," you say, "you're suggesting I take money *out* of the fund that's doing well and put it *into* the fund that's going down?"

Yes, that's exactly what I'm suggesting.

"Are you crazy?!" you ask.

Nope.

"Why in the world would I want to do that???" you wonder.

Because the basic principles of asset allocation and dollar cost averaging work. But they only work if you apply them. Here's why.

First, keep in mind that the reason you diversify in the first place is because no one can time the market—we never know for sure when a given asset class is about to go up or down—but we do know that different types of stocks tend to move in different directions. Your small-cap value fund may be going up now, and it may continue to grow. But what happens if it reaches, say, 50% of the total value of your portfolio, and then suddenly crashes? You'd take a huge hit to fully half of your retirement fund.

Second, when that developed countries fund loses value, you have an opportunity to buy more shares of it at a bargain price, because you're investing every single month. The power of dollar cost averaging lies, in part, in your ability to buy more shares at the lower price. Then, when the market turns, as it inevitably will, and that developed countries fund starts to do better, you'll own more shares of it, and you'll reap the benefits of the increasing value of all those shares. You can't reap the full benefit, though, if your allocation to that fund has dwindled to 5% of your portfolio.

In that scenario it's easy to see why sticking to the fundamentals works to your advantage. But keeping your portfolio in the proper balance is key to making it all come together. Rebalancing it on a regular basis is an essential part of your investment strategy. Do it quarterly if possible, or at the very least every year.

CAN YOU HANDLE IT ALL YOURSELF? SHOULD YOU?

By now you've got an excellent understanding of a few basic principles that can make you a very successful investor—in fact, they can make you More than a Millionaire. The principles are simple enough...in theory. I admit, though, applying them can become a bit complicated when you're new to investing, and even when you have years of experience.

There's an easy solution to that. While it's important—I would argue it's even essential—that you understand these strategies yourself, there are a number of reasons why it makes sense to consider hiring a financial advisor to help you implement them. As we've said before, this is your financial future we're talking about. You have a lot at stake. Why not enlist the help of an expert, someone whose life's work is all about helping people like you apply these strategies and realize your goals?

You can do it all on your own if you like. But I suggest you give some serious thought to working with a pro—but not just anyone with an office and a business card. Let me show you what an advisor can and cannot do for you, and what it takes to find one you can trust, who can help you make more money than you could on your own.

Then you can decide for yourself what's best for you.

CHAPTER 15

 FIND AN ADVISOR TO HELP YOU

Last summer I attended a picnic to celebrate the retirement of one of my long-term clients. Or maybe I should say he was celebrating his new-found freedom. He was all smiles when he described the vacation home he and his wife were thinking of buying out on the lake. And his eyes sparkled as he told me about plans to take his grandkids to Europe over spring break. I could tell he was already savoring the wonderful memories he'd be able to create with his family.

"You know, Randy," he said, "there was a time when I thought it was just an impossible dream to think I'd ever have the opportunity to do things like this. But now...it's all happening. I couldn't be happier."

As the party was winding down, I wandered over to where my client's son, Matthew, and a couple of his buddies were finishing off the last few beers from the cooler. They were having a friendly debate about the pros and cons of hiring a financial advisor to handle their money as they were building their own retirement funds. They were all hard-working, sensible young men, with varying degrees of commitment to building retirement accounts for themselves. But now that they were seeing Matt's dad actually reap the rewards of a lifetime of careful financial planning, they were inspired to get serious about making sure there would be similar celebrations in their own futures. They all agreed they were going to make it a priority. What they couldn't agree on was whether or not they should hire a financial advisor to help them invest their money, as Matt's dad had done.

"Okay, Randy," Matthew began as I twisted the cap off the last cold bottle of iced tea, "I know my way around different types of investments. But I know my dad is convinced he wouldn't be where he is today if you hadn't been there to handle his retirement account. He's even said he never would have been able to send me to college without your help. But seriously...what can an advisor do for me that I can't do for myself?"

"It's a great question, Matthew," I answered. "A good advisor can save you a lot of time and worry, improve your return on your investments, and even save you money on taxes. But a bad financial advisor can get you in a lot of trouble, and potentially put your financial future in serious jeopardy. So while you're deciding whether or not you need the help of an expert, make sure you also consider what it will take to find one who will help you—not hurt you."

"But don't financial advisors have to have a license to be in business?" asked Mike. He and Matthew had been roommates in college, and they now worked at the same marketing firm downtown. They were pretty competitive, but they always had each other's backs. "I would think the government would regulate that sort of thing pretty closely. Don't they need to have a lot of training before they can manage people's money?"

I shook my head. "Not necessarily. And even if they do have a lot of training, it doesn't mean they understand how to invest your money in a way that's consistent with your goals, while getting you a reasonable return over the many years you'll be investing, with a reasonable level of risk. Even worse, it doesn't mean they always have your best interest at heart."

Matthew had a worried look on his face. "I don't get it. Isn't the whole point of being a financial advisor to help clients make money?"

"For the good advisors, it is," I said. "But think about it. How does the advisor get paid? Some earn most of their money by getting a commission on selling you a particular kind of investment. In that scenario, will his recommendations be designed to make money for you, or for him? And even if he really is in it to make sure you do well, if he doesn't have enough experience to understand how to handle the ups and downs of the stock market, he could make mistakes that leave you moving shopping carts around at Wal-Mart when you're 75 years old."

Matt and his buddies exchanged a look and shifted in their seats. Michael took a long, slow drink of his beer.

Kevin, the youngest and most serious of the three, looked me straight in the eye. "Mr. Thurman," he said, "what are the odds of finding an advisor with good intentions, the right training, and plenty of experience?"

Now it was my turn to take a slow, cool drink of my tea, just to ease the knot in my stomach. I wasn't comfortable with what I had to tell these young men. "I'm sorry to tell you this, fellas, but I'd have to say your odds are about one in fifty."

Michael let out a long whistle. Kevin just shook his head.

Matthew set his beer down hard on the table. "Wait," he said, "just two percent of advisors can do the kind of job you'd recommend? You've got to be kidding me."

"I'm afraid I'm not, Matt."

"Then are you suggesting we'd be better off to do without an advisor?" he asked.

"No, not necessarily. Some investors can do fine on their own, but there are lots of reasons to consider hiring a professional to help you with some of the most important financial decisions you'll ever make. The thing is, if you decide you do want to use an advisor, the very best advice I can give you is to do your homework and find one of those rare individuals who meets three basic criteria. First he needs to have enough training and experience to know what he's doing. Second, he needs to be honest, the kind of guy you can actually trust with your money, the kind of person who will tell you the truth, even when you don't want to hear it. Finally, you need someone who is genuinely in it to help you, who will do everything possible to make sure you have a great outcome."

So...what's the right choice for you? Should you go it alone, or find one of those one-in-fifty advisors who will help you make your More than a Millionaire goals a reality? If you decide to get help, how will you know if you've found the right person for the job?

In this chapter we'll tackle all three of those questions. Then, in case you decide you do want to enlist the help of an advisor, I'll give you seven questions to ask to make sure the one you hire is a great one.

Do You Really Need an Advisor?

Even if you're the independent type who likes to travel solo, I encourage you to give some serious consideration to finding an expert to be your guide. Think about it: If you're about to set out on a remote mountain path you've never been on before, wouldn't it be helpful to have input from a local who knows all the most scenic—and safest—routes? Someone you can call if you find yourself on a narrow trail with a steep drop-off, wondering if it's safe to continue on around the bend, or smarter to backtrack and find an easier climb?

A good financial advisor is a lot like that local guide, because he's been down that path before. He can warn you about the risks ahead, and also help you know which risks are worth taking. And, metaphors aside, if you've made it this far into this book, you now know enough about investing to realize how much there is to learn—

with the likely conclusion that expert advice would itself be a good investment.

A great advisor will benefit you much more, over time, than he costs. Here are some of the more significant things he or she can do for you:

- Create a well-diversified portfolio, with assets allocated in a way that makes sense for you, at this stage in your life as an investor and given your unique circumstances and goals, to give you the best opportunity for an excellent return without excessive risk

- Rebalance your portfolio on a regular basis, to make sure the asset allocation remains consistent with the strategy you've chosen as best suited to your needs (See "Rebalancing" on page 216 in Chapter 14.)

- Monitor the mutual funds you've invested in, to make sure they're managed properly and continue to provide the types of assets you need in your portfolio

- Help you make decisions rationally rather than emotionally, and prevent you from buying or selling assets based on emotion

- Prevent you from making The Big Mistake—like trying to hit a home run by finding a hot stock or second-guessing which way the market is going—and blowing it (The Big Mistake could set you back years of investment growth, or even derail your retirement plans altogether.)

- Help you manage your investments in a way that minimizes the amount of taxes you have to pay
- Save you a ton of time by helping you handle all of the above

Now, if you have the time, temperament, and talent to do all these things yourself, you may want to go it alone. But expert assistance with *any single* item on this list can easily be worth the fees you'll pay to an advisor.

Advisors, generally speaking, add value. Studies have shown that the *average* advisor—not a star, mind you, just an average, middle of the road kind of guy—will increase your investment return relative to what you would have done on your own. But will it really be enough of an increase to offset what you'll pay him?

Of course I can't make any guarantees, but there's a ton of evidence out there that says it will. One long-term study looked at a group of people investing on their own over a period of 20 years. The analysis found that if those investors had been working with an advisor, they would have paid him on average about 1% of the amount they had invested—but their annual return would have improved by an average of 6%.[50] That's a net gain of about 5% per year. Just imagine the impact that extra 5%, year after year after year, would have on your portfolio over the next 30 years. No doubt about it, that would make a dramatic difference in your quality of life in retirement.

---

[50] Nick Murray, *Behavorial Investment Counseling*, Mattituck, NY: The Nick Murray Company, Inc., 2008.

Here's the thing. If your advisor does nothing more than help you keep emotion out of the decision-making process, he'll probably earn his keep on that basis alone. That's because, of all of the things an advisor can do for you, what's most important is his ability to help you calm your nerves when times are tough and you want to bail, and also to keep you grounded when things are great and you want to invest more aggressively. He'll keep you from selling everything when the stock market is tanking (which it inevitably will from time to time), and also keep you from putting all your eggs in one basket when the Dow Jones—or a particular segment of the market—soars. Bottom line, an advisor will help you develop your investment strategy and then stick to it, which is one of the toughest things to do if you're going solo. That alone will increase the probability that, no matter what happens in the outside world, you'll be able to achieve your goal of becoming More than a Millionaire.

That's what your average, run-of-the-mill advisor can do for you. But what if you can find an advisor who's not just average, but really great at what he does? Imagine the possibilities. By asking the right questions you can find someone who meets our three criteria: He's knowledgeable, he's trustworthy, and he cares about you.

How to Find a Great Advisor

The first step in finding an advisor is to put together a list of candidates worth considering. In this day and age of everything-online, it may be tempting to sign up for a web-based service. I would highly discourage this. If you had a serious illness (as serious as, say, your financial future), would you want to get a diagnosis and treatment online, from someone who doesn't know you? Will someone working for a web-based service take the time to get to know your history, your concerns, your goals? Will he be there when you're about to make The Big Mistake?

Your financial future is too important to trust it to some anonymous person out there in cyberland. Find someone who works in your community, so you can sit down in her office and look her in the eye. You want someone who will take your unique circumstances into account, and tailor a strategy that's suited to you—not just hand over a boilerplate plan designed for people who may or may not be anything like you. Besides, someone with roots in your community is more likely to have a vested interest in maintaining long-term relationships with her clients, which of course means doing a great job for them.

Start by getting referrals from people you trust, people who have some experience investing their own money. If you know someone who's just retired with a nice nest egg (like Matthew's dad, who you met at the beginning of this chapter), find out who his advisor is. If you have a retirement plan at work, talk to the person who administers the plan. You can also gather a preliminary list of names by visiting the websites of organizations that oversee credentials for financial planners. Most include a tool for finding an advisor in your area. Go to www.CFP.net, www.AICPA.org (type "find a CPA/PFS" in the "Search" box, and click the link), or www.NAPFA.org.

Seven questions to ask

Once you have a list of local advisors that come well recommended, it's time to do your own research to narrow it down until you find the best one for you. I've put together a list of questions that will help you determine whether each advisor meets our three key criteria:

1. Is he competent?
2. Can you trust her?
3. Does he have your interest at heart?

You can find answers to many of the questions that follow just by going online and visiting the advisors' websites. It's fine to use that information for your initial screening process, mostly to rule out candidates who clearly don't meet your criteria. But once that's done, there's no substitute for having a face-to-face conversation with each advisor on your short list, for reasons that will become clear as we take a closer look at the questions you'll be asking.

1. IS HE COMPETENT?

Competence is about knowledge, and having the technical skills to do the job. A financial advisor acquires knowledge and skill by undergoing initial training in his field, then applying that training through years of on-the-job experience. He maintains his expertise by participating in continuing education opportunities throughout his career. Here are a few questions that will help you determine whether the advisor you're considering is competent.

"What professional credentials have you earned?"

There's a fairly long list of credentials an advisor can tack on to his name—some are essential, others are fairly meaningless. Some credentials represent formal education in the field, others merely indicate an affiliation with a particular organization. You should only consider those candidates who have earned *recognized* professional qualifications to manage your money.

He should have *at least one* of the following credentials:

- CFP® – Certified Financial Planner™
- CPA/PFS – Certified Public Accountant with a Personal Financial Specialist designation

The organizations that grant these designations require the applicant to pass an initial exam. He must also obtain continuing professional education. While that doesn't guarantee an advisor is competent, a planner with one or both of these credentials has made a commitment to a minimum amount of training and ongoing education, or he can't keep the designation.

A college degree, and preferably an MBA (Master's degree in Business Administration) with an emphasis in finance, is also nice. Just like the professional designations, it does not prove competence, but it does indicate an ability to use analytical skills required in this profession. It suggests a good foundation for the professional courses and continuing education studies.

Be aware, too, that some designations are virtually meaningless. There are close to 200 different designations and letters financial planners can attach to their names, some of which require nothing more than a modest fee to use them. A large brokerage company has recently come under fire for creating their own designation just to make their brokers look better. Beware!

And, of course, you need to confirm all designations and degrees by calling the organizations that confer them. Beginning on page 240, near the end of this chapter, you'll find a summary of the alphabet soup of designations, along with phone numbers for the regulatory bodies that govern them. Anyone can put letters after his name on a website or a business card—that doesn't necessarily mean he's earned them. Protect yourself by taking the time to verify that your advisor has the credentials he claims he does.

"How much financial planning and investment advisory experience do you have?"

As a rule of thumb, consider only planners who have been around long enough to have experience handling the inevitable downturns in the market, as well as the times when things are going well. Typically the market goes through a major slide every three to five years, but sometimes the good times last even longer. Many younger advisors just don't have enough time on the job to have experienced all of that, so they may not be seasoned enough to be able to help you ride out those highs and lows.

At the same time, you're looking for an advisor who will be with you for the long haul. Someone who is sixty-five years old when you meet him probably won't be working ten or fifteen years from now. You don't want to have to start all over again with someone new, just when your portfolio is really growing into a substantial amount of money.

I suggest you find someone who has a *minimum* of five years' experience, preferably ten—but also who is not more than five years older than you are. That will give you a reasonable chance he'll have the experience you need, and also be around to see you through a majority of your years as an investor.

"How do you keep up with the ongoing changes in the financial environment?"
In other words, how many hours of continuing education does he take? If he takes the minimum, how is he going to be better than the other advisors? You want him to say he takes around 50 or more hours (clock hours) of course work each year.

You might even want to ask for a list of the courses the advisor has taken over last two years. This should be easy for him to get for you, and it will give you an idea whether his areas of interest and study reflect your needs and circumstances. If *all* his courses are devoted to managing multi-million-dollar accounts, he might be the best advisor on the planet for people in those demographics. But his course selection might indicate he's less than excited about working with someone like you, when you're just getting started, and perhaps not quite up to speed on the latest research or investment opportunities that are important for you.

Let me assure you, this is important information. There is no way on earth anyone can be excellent at planning unless he or she is committed to staying current on financial issues, particularly those that impact you the most.

2. CAN YOU TRUST HER?

It goes without saying that a "trusted" advisor should be fundamentally honest, should not be a felon (Don't laugh—you know they're out there!), and should not have an army of angry clients filing complaints against her. She should also be free of obligations to promote investments that benefit anyone other than you. That means she recommends investment opportunities that are right for you, rather than pushing products that earn her a big commission or that meet some kind of quota set up by the company she works for.

Do a background check.

The first step in evaluating the trustworthiness of any potential advisor is to do a background check. Nope, this one isn't a question. I wouldn't bother asking a candidate about this one directly. It goes without saying (doesn't it?) that someone who has stolen from clients or anyone else, or who has misled or otherwise treated clients badly, is not likely to fess up about it to you. The only reliable way to get the truth is to do your own research. It may sound like overkill, but believe me—this *is* a requirement. Check with the Securities and Exchange Commission (SEC, www.sec.gov, 800-SEC-0330) for advisors, and the Financial Industry Regulating Authority (FINRA, www.FINRA.org, 301-590-6500) for registered representatives, which is someone who can sell securities on commission. (Be sure to read *carefully* my cautionary info, on page 236, about people who work on commission.) The FINRA website has a nice "BrokerCheck" button on its home page that allows you to check out the registered representatives in your area. There are also state securities agencies for registered representatives or advisors who work on a smaller scale, and state insurance regulators who license insurance agents. If you google your state's name, along with "department of securities" or "department of insurance," you'll find contact information for the appropriate regulating agencies where you can verify credentials and check for complaints or violations.

Let's be realistic. It's tough for any professional to deal with the general public for five or ten years and not have any complaints. But if your planner has been convicted of a felony or is not currently licensed, you absolutely have to find out now. Use your biggest, boldest Sharpie to cross her off your list.

"Does your firm sell any of its own products?"

Many firms require their representatives to offer company products first, even if a better investment is available. In fact, in some cases in-house products are the only options they can recommend. They may also be compensated heavily for selling those in-house products. It's pretty tough, even for someone who's fundamentally honest, to resist the urge to push a product that earns her a nice bonus, whether or not it's the right investment for you.

This is obviously not on the scale of felonious behavior, but it's a killer for most brokers. Beware of those whose first priority is to move their company's products! If the answer to this question is yes, then you don't need to ask any other questions. Move on to the next advisor.

Let me very clear: *Trustworthiness is critical.*

3. DOES HE HAVE YOUR INTEREST AT HEART?

At first glance, it may seem that this is a tricky one to pin down. How can you possibly tell, early on in any relationship, if someone genuinely cares about you?

I have three words for you: Follow the money. It won't tell you everything you need to know, but knowing how an advisor makes his own money will give you a clue to where his loyalty lies. You also need to know whether the two of you are on the same page regarding your approach to investing. It's true that you're looking for an expert who knows far more about these matters than you do. But you can't just hand over your financial future to an advisor and assume his vision for your success is consistent with your own.

You don't need to be an expert yourself to find out whether a potential advisor will have your back, and be committed to helping you become More than a Millionaire. You just need to know what questions to ask, such as...

"How do you get paid?"

No one works for free. Financial advisors get paid, primarily, in one of two ways. Either they get paid on *commission* every time they buy or sell a stock or bond or other investment vehicle, or they get paid a *fee*—that can be an hourly rate, or a flat fee paid at regular intervals, or a percentage based on the size of your portfolio. Commissions are paid by the company the advisor works for. A fee is paid by the client...theoretically, you. Right from the start, that should give you some indication of where an advisor's loyalties are likely be: Who pays his salary, the company or you?

If the advisor gets paid on commission, you should be cautious. It'll be tough for him to be loyal to you if his income comes from someone else. Unless you have a strong reason to do otherwise, I suggest you move on.

Stick with the advisors who charge a fee. Typically they'll charge you a percentage of the assets they manage for you, usually between 0.9% and 1.5% per year. The larger your portfolio, the smaller your fee percentage is likely to be, because they make more money based on the volume of assets. With this compensation method the planner does better when you do better, because when your assets increase, his income increases. It also works the other way—when the value of your account drops, his income goes down. He also makes more money if he can keep you happy for years to come. A fee-based arrangement fosters a long-term relationship between you and the advisor, and a financial incentive for him to have your best interest at heart.

You can see that, when an advisor's fee is based on a percentage of your assets, his income is closely tied to the amount of money in your account. That means there's not much in it for him when you're just starting out as an investor. 1.5% of a few thousand dollars doesn't amount to much for the amount of work he'll put in. In that scenario you'll probably pay a flat fee, probably around $1,000 to

$1,500 a year. Or you might pay your advisor on an hourly basis, generally between $100 and $400 an hour.

Another option may be to use your parents' advisor, if they have one, and place your account under the umbrella of their account. You'll likely be charged the lower percentage based on the total amount of assets in both accounts. If that's available to you, chances are it would be less costly than going it alone.

"How will you invest my money?"

A good financial plan starts with…a plan. But there's no cookie-cutter plan that works for everyone. A good plan can take many forms. It can be a list of action steps on a legal pad, all the way up to a thick set of charts and graphs. One is not necessarily better than the other. It depends on how detailed your needs are and what kind of experience your advisor has. Even if the written plan is short, the advisor's fact finding about you should be thorough. The planner should ask you about your retirement goals, look at your tax return, talk about risk and how you feel about it, show you some portfolios, and more. What's most critical here is that the plan should be tailored to your needs.

You also need to know how your potential advisor makes decisions about where to put your money. Does he follow a strategy for asset allocation similar to the portfolio I described on page 213 in Chapter 14? If not, why not? Does his explanation make sense to you?

If he doesn't stick to a long-term strategy of asset allocation, what does he base his decisions on? Does he try to pick the "hot stock of the week"? Does he try to anticipate trends in one market sector, like tech stocks, or another? Does he claim he can get a big return with no risk? (This can't be done. If he says he can do it...*Run!*)

Your goal is to find an advisor who follows a prudent, long-term investment strategy, who listens to your goals and develops a sound plan for achieving them, and who applies sound principles of asset allocation.

Once you've established that the advisor meets those criteria, there are just a few more things you should expect him to do for you.

- The advisor should discuss with you the expected rates of return for your portfolio, and what it will look like in those times when the market takes a hit, which it inevitably will. That way, when tough times come along, you'll be prepared.

- The advisor should be willing and able to purchase the various asset classes you've chosen for your portfolio using no-load mutual funds, which are funds you can buy and sell without paying a sales fee.

- The advisor should be prepared to rebalance your portfolio periodically—preferably quarterly.

- Finally, the advisor should be willing to put all these elements in writing in an investment policy statement. This statement should provide specific instructions and cover such topics as target rates of return, the level of risk you're comfortable with, what percentage of the portfolio will be held in each asset class, and rebalancing.

"What happens if it doesn't work out?"

The benefits you receive from hiring an advisor should outweigh the cost. In case they don't, find out what costs you'll incur if you want to get out of the arrangement. A relatively small fee—say $200 or less—is common. But it doesn't make sense to pay a large "get out" fee, as my dad would call it. If an advisor uses fees as coercion to keep you as a client, it should send up a serious red flag. Look for an advisor who practices good money management as an incentive to keep you happy. A carrot is always better than a stick.

FINANCIAL ADVISOR ALPHABET SOUP

"What do all those letters really mean?"

The following is a glossary of credentials and affiliations you'll run across in your search for a truly great financial advisor. I've included contact information you can use to verify whether the advisor you're considering has in fact earned and maintained the right to use a given credential as he claims.

CFA – Chartered Financial Analyst. This is a fairly prestigious credential held primarily by institutional money managers and stock analysts. It is issued after several years of appropriate work experience and rigorous testing by the Association for Investment Management and Research in Charlottesville, Virginia. Contact: www.CFAinstitute.org, (804) 980-3668.

CFP® – Certified Financial Planner™. The credential is issued by the Certified Financial Planner Board of Standards in Denver, a nongovernmental organization. An applicant must complete five topic-specific exams and then a comprehensive exam, and agrees to abide by a code of ethics. A person who has a CFP® is serious about the profession. Out of all the designations, this is the one I would recommend as most essential for the advisor you ultimately hire. Contact: www.CFP.net, (800) 487-1497.

CPA – Certified Public Accountant. A CPA must pass an extensive, rigorous test administered nationally, and receive approval from state accountancy boards. CPAs are trained to work in many areas.

Optimally, the ones that can help you manage your investments will also have the PFS designation (see below). This is a designation specifically for CPAs helping clients in the area of personal financial planning. To confirm that a CPA has an active license, go to: www.CPAverify.org. Or, for more research options, you can contact the appropriate State Board of Accountancy where the individual obtained his or her license. There is a complete list of contact information for each state board located at this website address: http://www.aicpa.org/Advocacy/State/StateContactInfo/Pages/StateContactInformation.aspx. Click on the state, then click on the link to that state's accountancy board website. Each site should have a link that says "Find a CPA" or something similar.

CPA/PFS – Certified Public Accountant, Personal Financial Specialist. The Personal Financial Specialist (PFS) program allows CPAs to demonstrate their knowledge and expertise in personal financial planning. CPA/PFS credential holders have specific experience, education, and examination requirements that set them apart from other CPAs and financial planners. This is a really outstanding designation. To find one in your area, go to www.AICPA.org, type "find a CPA/PFS" in the "Search" box, and click the link. Or if you prefer, call the AICPA at (888) 777-7077.

MBA – Master of Business Administration. This graduate-level degree is generally seen as an indication of a solid background in financial matters. Call the university indicated on the advisor's degree to confirm its validity.

NAPFA – The National Association of Personal Financial Advisors. NAPFA is the country's leading professional association of fee-only financial advisors—highly trained professionals who are committed to working in the best interests of those they serve. The organization has been helping people find fee-only advisors since 1983. Contact: www.NAPFA.org, (888) 333-6659 (or 888-FEE-ONLY).

RIA – Registered Investment Advisor. Not a credential, it simply means an individual or a firm has submitted certain filings with the Securities and Exchange Commission (SEC), and the individual has passed an exam, paid a modest fee, and is held to a higher standard of responsibility and accountability. An RIA or an RIA firm is a fiduciary and required to put the client's interests first. In my opinion you should always use an RIA or an Investment Advisor Representative (IAR) from an RIA firm. To check on this, go to www.adviserinfo.sec.gov and enter the advisor's name in the search box. When his name shows up in the search results, click "Get Details" to get the full report.

RR – Registered Representative. This refers to a person who has passed one or more securities exams, and who is regulated by the Financial Industry Regulatory Authority, more commonly known as FINRA. There is no explicit financial-planning component to the testing. *This is also not a professional designation* but part of the licensing required *to sell* securities on a commission basis.

Unfortunately the exams cover a lot of stuff most advisors will never use in a lifetime in the securities business. They're difficult tests, but the knowledge base they cover is so very broad it is probably not going to help you in the areas most important to you. FINRA maintains a database of all licensees, any complaints that have been lodged against them, and how those complaints have been resolved. In some cases complaints are minor, or the agency has determined a complaint was unfounded. In any case, it's a good idea to check. Contact: www.FINRA.org, (301) 590-6500.

CHAPTER 16

 18 TRAITS OF THE HAPPY AND WEALTHY

Financial success leaves clues. I teach a seminar on the traits of wealthy people, based on my experience studying them for more than three decades—and I've always been particularly interested in those who became wealthy starting from scratch. After one seminar, an attendee said to me, "If I was wealthy, I would have more of these traits." I think she had it backwards—if she'd had more of these traits, she would have been more likely to be wealthy.

The habits you develop, the beliefs you hold about yourself and the world around you, and the way you respond to life's challenges all affect your ability to accumulate wealth. Many assume financial independence is something you inherit. In reality, far more people become wealthy because of their own choices and habits than as a result of inheritance. In his book *The Millionaire Next Door: The Surprising Secrets of America's Wealthy*, acclaimed researcher Thomas Stanley, Ph.D., tells us that more than 80% of the millionaires in America today inherited little or none of their money from ancestors; they accumulated their wealth over the course of their own lives.

At the same time, by now you know I firmly believe it's not just about wealth, but about happiness as well. Throughout this book I have shared some of my views about the philosophy of money, and about the reasons why I think becoming wealthy is a worthy goal. But what good is it to gain the world if you're unhappy?

My goal is to help you attain both material wealth and happiness. And so, before we conclude our time together, I'd like to share a little more about the philosophy and traits that are common among people who are wealthy *and* happy.

CULTIVATE HAPPINESS AND WEALTH: HOW MANY OF THESE TRAITS DO YOU HAVE?

1. *The happy and wealthy are disciplined.*

In a recent study, when millionaires were asked what traits are most important for attaining success, discipline was at the top of the list.[51]

If you plan to save $10 a day, and the day rolls by and you don't have the discipline to save that $10, you can say, "Heh, it's only one day." Disaster starts to set in when you do that time and time again, and say, "No harm done." Those days add up to weeks, weeks turn into months, months become years, and years become a lifetime.

And as my dad has told me many times, "Son, it don't take long to live a lifetime."

---

[51] Thomas Stanley, *The Millionaire Mind*, Kansas City, MO: Andrews McMeel Publishing, 2001.

Discipline is the bridge between learning the information in the pages of this book and realizing your goals. It is the foundation of all financial success. Without it there is no long-term success.

2. *The wealthy tend to save first, then spend what's left. Those who make money but do not become wealthy tend to spend first, then save what's left.*

When I talk with people who make $25,000 a year, they tell me it takes every dollar they make just to live. Probably so.

When I talk to those who make $30,000 a year, they also tell me it takes everything to live.

What happened to the extra $5,000?

If the people who make $30,000 decide to live like those who make $25,000, and start doing it when they're young enough, they can become financially independent later in life—and even be able to help others do so as well. Financial independence does not come from making and having "enough" money. It's the result of the choices you make early in life.

And it's never too late to get started, because "today" is always earlier than never.

3. *The happy and wealthy are granite splitters.*

What do I mean by that? They are persistent even when there seems to be no progress.

I recently saw a YouTube video of a guy splitting a piece of granite. I'm not sure how many blows he made on that thing, but let's say it was hundreds, without any visible progress. Zip, nada, none.

Yet he kept at it, and finally there was one blow where this large piece of granite split in two. It wasn't because of that one blow—it was the result of all that had come before it.

The wealthy are persistent and stay true to their goals even when there appears to be little or no progress. They don't give up. They're persistent—not only for themselves, but for those around them as well.

4. *The happy and wealthy think in longer time frames.*

This is a critical one. Those who make money but never get ahead tend to think in terms of how they will get by this month, this week, or today. Wealthy people tend to ask, "Where do I want to be in 10 years, or in 15 or 20 years?" They even ask, "How do I want to impact future generations?"

When you think only about what you want today, you come up with options that are very different from what you find when you think about what you want to have in ten years. Taking that educational class for self-improvement makes no sense whatsoever if you're thinking about having fun today. Setting aside $100 each month doesn't make sense, either, if you'd rather be having a double latte every workday.

The happy and wealthy tend to value having financial options and financial freedom over immediate comfort. Because they do, they tend to get both. Many who do not achieve financial freedom value immediate comfort over freedom and control. Because they do, they eventually get neither.

The wealthy think in terms of longer time frames, and ask, "What do I need to do to get there?"

5. *The wealthy invest differently.*

They invest in stocks, bonds, and mutual funds, and they understand the ups and downs that go along with investing. They may invest in real estate or in their own businesses. They think long term, and short-term fluctuations don't bother them (too much). They know that, over time, these investments should yield a higher return. Those who make money but never accumulate much tend to invest in guaranteed investments with returns that never fluctuate, not even in the short run. They see short term fluctuation as a loss, and tend not to give much weight to the value of returns over the long run.

6. *The wealthy play by the tax rules, but they work the rules very hard.*

The happy and wealthy understand the tax laws, or they find someone who can help them apply the tax laws wisely. They are firm believers in legal tax *avoidance*—not tax *evasion*, but implementing legal strategies to pay the minimum amount of tax. For example, they contribute to before tax, tax-deferred retirement plans almost without exception. They compare the costs and benefits of each tax strategy and make choices accordingly. Those who don't accumulate much wealth tend to pay their taxes as they go, and feel that implementing strategies to minimize the amount they pay is not worth the hassle, or that it's too difficult to learn and too much trouble to get help.

7. *The wealthy keep track of how they're progressing toward their goals.*

They monitor their progress in all areas of their lives, because they know that when you keep score, the score tends to improve. The wealthy and happy know where they are on their personal road to success.

They apply that principle to their financial lives by utilizing tools like spending plans and net worth statements. They know where they are and where they want to be, and have the numbers to prove it.

8. *The happy and wealthy evaluate life events differently.*

They use the past as a school, not an anchor. In Tony Robbins' book *Awaken the Giant Within: How to Take Control of Your Mental, Emotional, Physical, and Financial Destiny*, he shares a story about two sons born to a father who was an alcoholic. Dad was a mean man, especially when he was drunk. Eventually he was thrown in jail for the murder of a liquor store cashier.

Dad had two sons. One grew up to be just like his dad, a mean drunk who went through his life stealing and threatening others until he, too, was thrown in jail. The other son grew up to be a model of success, happy in most things, successful and significant.

When both sons were asked, "Why has your life turned out this way?" they gave the same answer: "How else could it have turned out, having a dad like that?" One used their father as an excuse; one used him as a lesson in what not to do.

The wealthy learn from the mistakes of others. They also make mistakes of their own, but they correct their courses and move on.

You, too, can correct your course. You may not be able to change where you are overnight. But at any moment you can change your direction—and your destination.

9. The happy and wealthy don't see failure as failure, but as a learning experience.

I used to volunteer coaching soccer...for 8-year-olds. Once, one of my players let the other team get by him, and they scored. He was dejected, and said, "I failed."

Seeing this as a teachable moment, I said, "Never see failure as failure, but as a learning experience!"

To which he replied, "I must be learning a whole lot this game!"

Be like my soccer player. Learn a lot and use it.

Never see failure as failure but as a learning experience. Try hard, learn from what happens, improve, move forward.

10. The happy and wealthy tend to value financial independence over social status.

Will Rogers said, "Too many people spend money they haven't earned, to buy things they don't want, to impress people they don't like." He was right.

My dad puts it a different way. He says, "Big hat, but no cattle." What he means is, many people try to look the part to impress others, but they have no substance.

Have substance, and let the others show off. A typical happy and wealthy person will spend 60% to 70% of her budget on living a comfortable, enjoyable life. The rest goes to charity, investing, debt reduction, or education.

11. *The wealthy and happy take responsibility for their happiness as well as their financial situation.*

They don't blame the government, the cost of things, taxes, Democrats, Republicans, or anyone else for failure or disappointments. They take responsibility for their lives.

They know things happen that they can't control, but they also know they can control how they react to those things. Setbacks will happen—but there's always more than one way to respond, and some responses are clearly more positive than others. The wealthy and happy seek to learn from difficult circumstances, and they recognize that they will always feel better afterward when they have reacted well.

12. *The happy and wealthy tend to be highly motivated to do well.*

Often their motivation comes from a particular life experience. Perhaps they grew up poor and did without. Or perhaps they dream of retiring in a special place and work toward that.

Whatever the reason, they have a vision of what life should be like, and they're driven to make that vision a reality.

13. *The happy and wealthy believe in constant improvement.*

The happy and wealthy want to get better; they want to be better. They study, read, talk to mentors, get special training and certification. They strive to be the best they can be at the work they do and in other areas that are important in their lives. If becoming wealthy is important to them, they study how to become wealthy. If happiness is important to them, they study happiness.

14. *The happy and wealthy believe personal integrity comes first.*

When the happy and wealthy are in a situation that requires them to choose between adhering to their values and making money, they will choose adhering to their values every time. Because they do, in the long run they attract the type of people who help them become more successful.

The happy and wealthy feel that wealth without character is worthless.

15. *The happy and wealthy spend more than most people on memorable experiences.*

The happy and wealthy understand it's not all about dying with the most chips. They're willing to spend a portion of their wealth on life experiences, to create fond memories for themselves and those they care about. They go on trips, spend time and money on things they enjoy, and build a trove of memorable times they share with loved ones.

They also don't want to be 80 (or whatever age) and be a burden to their families. It's about balance, and they tend to find a healthy balance in this thing called life.

16. *The happy and wealthy, contrary to popular opinion, tend to be generous.*

At least that's true of the ones I've been around. Interestingly enough, they were even generous before they were wealthy. As a general rule, it was a habit that began when they were just starting out. They were grateful for what they had—even when they didn't have much—and they shared what they had with others.

That's one of the reasons they're not just wealthy, but also happy.

17. *The happy and wealthy are a little lucky.*

Yes, they are. As a general rule, they had some breaks along the way. Often they'll tell you they have been fortunate. They will also tell you—and firmly believe—that the harder you work, the luckier you get.

Now, there's really no way to work on just being lucky. But you can certainly work on working smart and hard to achieve your goals. When you do, you might find a little more luck coming your way.

18. *The happy and wealthy strive for significance.*

They strive to go beyond the dictionary definition of success. They want to make a significant, lasting, positive difference in other people's lives.

The happy and wealthy strive to contribute something that extends beyond their own lives.

The Choice Is Yours

You're at a point in your life where you have a vast array of options available to you. It's probably obvious that you have some hefty decisions to make—about your job, about marriage and family, about where you live, and more—any of which may have a profound impact on how your life unfolds in the years to come.

But perhaps the greatest choice of all is about *how* you live your life. I'm referring to the values you choose as guideposts, the beliefs you adopt and incorporate into your worldview, and the habits you adopt and integrate into your daily routine.

Each and every choice you make today helps set the direction of your life going forward. And since the tiniest adjustment in that direction can radically alter the trajectory of your journey, and so where you'll find yourself 30, 40, or 50 years from now, it's wise to make sure every choice you make keeps you headed someplace you really want to go.

Choosing to adopt the habits of people who have gone before you to the places you want to go is one way to ensure a successful journey for yourself. I know you'll choose wisely.

Appendix

Your Three-Year Reading Plan for Success

"You're where you are in life primarily because of the books you read and the people you know."

–Jim Rohn, Success Coach

Become an avid reader. With audio books today, e-books, and easy access to printed books, there is no reason not to. I have read more than 50 books a year for the last 25 years. I share that with you so you'll know that the list I recommend here is culled from more than a thousand titles, to what I believe are the 36 best secular books about success. They cover a broad range of topics including attitude, self-improvement, history, and of course a heavy emphasis on personal finance.[52]

Start a lifetime habit of reading one book a month. I promise you it will make a tremendous difference in the rest of your life.

---

[52] There's another long list of spiritual and religious books I value highly, and I feel it's incredibly important that you feed your life with books of that genre as well. Since there are so many ways to approach spirituality and religion, it's difficult to generate a list here that would be sure to resonate with your unique perspective. For that reason, and a few others, I've chosen to focus only on secular titles. I encourage you to add your own choices that will deepen and enrich your spiritual life in the years to come.

Year One.

1. *The Richest Man in Babylon*, George S. Clason
2. *The 10 Natural Laws of Successful Time and Life Management: Proven Strategies for Increased Productivity and Inner Peace*, Hyrum W. Smith
3. *The 7 Habits of Highly Effective People: Powerful Lessons in Personal Change*, Stephen R. Covey
4. *Man's Search for Meaning*, Viktor E. Frankl
5. *How to Win Friends and Influence People: The Only Book You Need to Lead You to Success*, Dale Carnegie
6. *Gaining Control: Your Key to Freedom and Success*, Robert F. Bennett
7. *Lessons of History*, Will & Ariel Durant
8. *First Things First*, Stephen R. Covey, A. Roger Merrill, & Rebecca R. Merrill
9. *Acres of Diamonds: All Good Things Are Possible, Right Where You Are, and Now!* Russell H. Conwell & Robert Shackleton
10. *The Power of Positive Thinking*, Norman Vincent Peale
11. *As a Man Thinketh*, James Allen
12. *Mastery: The Keys to Success and Long-Term Fulfillment*, George Leonard

Some of these books may take more than a month, others a couple of days. On average, read a book a month.

Year Two.

1. *Napoleon Hill's Keys to Success: The 17 Principles of Personal Achievement*, Napoleon Hill

2. *Happiness Advantage: The Seven Principles That Fuel Success and Performance at Work*, Shawn Achor

3. *Psychology of Persuasion: How to Persuade Others to Your Way of Thinking*, Kevin Hogan

4. *The Go-Giver: A Little Story About a Powerful Business Idea*, Bob Burg & John David Mann

5. *See You at the Top*, Zig Zigler

6. *My Philosophy for Successful Living*, Jim Rohn

7. *Economics in One Lesson: The Shortest and Surest Way to Understand Basic Economics*, Henry Hazlitt

8. *Simple Wealth, Inevitable Wealth*, Nick Murray

9. *The Total Money Makeover: A Proven Plan for Financial Fitness*, Dave Ramsey

10. *What to Say When You Talk to Yourself*, Shad Helmstetter

11. *What Got You Here Won't Get You There : How Successful People Become Even More Successful*, Marshall Goldsmith with Mark Reiter

12. *The Generosity Factor: Discover the Joy of Giving Your Time, Talent, and Treasure*, Ken Blanchard & S. Truett Cathy

13. *The Last Lecture*, Randy Pausch

I threw in the last book, #13, because it takes only about an hour to read.

Year Three.

1. *Think and Grow Rich*, Napoleon Hill
2. *Go-Givers Sell More*, Bob Burg & John David Mann
3. *Awaken the Giant Within: How to Take Immediate Control of Your Mental, Emotional, Physical and Financial Destiny!* Tony Robbins
4. *Influence: Science and Practice*, Robert B. Cialdini
5. *Who Moved My Cheese? An Amazing Way to Deal with Change in Your Work and in Your Life*, Spencer Johnson
6. *The One Minute Manager*, Ken Blanchard & Spencer Johnson
7. *Change Your Thinking, Change Your Life: How to Unlock Your Full Potential for Success and Achievement*, Brian Tracy
8. *Stumbling on Happiness*, Daniel Gilbert
9. *Why Smart People Make Big Money Mistakes and How to Correct Them: Lessons from the Life-Changing Science of Behavioral Economics*, Gary Belsky & Thomas Gilovich
10. *The Compound Effect: Jumpstart Your Income, Your Life, Your Success*, Darin Hardy
11. *Emotional Intelligence: Why It Can Matter More than IQ*, Daniel Goleman
12. *Thank You For Arguing: What Aristotle, Lincoln, and Homer Simpson Can Teach Us About the Art of Persuasion*, Jay Heinrichs

On top of this, I would watch, at the start of every year, Jim Rohn's DVD (also on YouTube) *How to Have Your Best Year Ever.*

About the Author

Randy L. Thurman started in the financial planning business in 1987, and has since become widely recognized as one of the top financial advisors in the United States. He specializes in helping those who have retired (or are about to retire) have a comfortable income for life. He is a Certified Public Accountant (CPA) and a CERTIFIED FINANCIAL PLANNER™ professional, also known as a CFP® professional. He is also a Personal Financial Specialist (PFS), a credential that recognizes CPAs with additional experience and expertise in financial planning. PFS candidates must pass a technical exam and complete rigorous continuing education requirements. Randy holds four degrees, including an MBA from Oklahoma State University, and has taught investing, personal finance, and economics at the college level.

In 1990 Randy founded his firm, Financial Planning Company of Oklahoma, which in 1997 merged with Retirement Investment Advisors, Inc. He continues today as president. Under his leadership the firm has become one of the largest fee-only investment advisory firms in Oklahoma where all advisors are CFP® professionals.

As a result of more than 30 years of dedication and commitment to excellence in financial planning, Randy is frequently lauded as one of the nation's most trusted investment advisors. As of this writing, he and his firm have been cited 31 times in national publications as among the best in the country. Accolades include:

- six times on *Worth* magazine's annual list of Top Financial Advisors in the country,
- six times on *Medical Economics'* list of Best Financial Advisors,
- seven times in *Bloomberg Wealth Manager Magazine*,
- four times in *Financial Times*,
- three times in *Financial Advisor Magazine*,
- twice in Best of the U.S. (web based),
- twice in J.K. Lasser's books on Estate Planning.

Randy has also been recognized on a local level for excellence and leadership, including:

- 2010 Oklahoma Business Ethics Compass Award,
- 2012 Oklahoma Society of CPAs award for Outstanding CPA in Financial Planning,
- 2013 *The Journal Record Beacon* Award, Charitable Influence – Small Business.

Over the years, Randy has shared his expertise and insight as the author of four books and an extensive list of articles on financial planning, investing, and business ethics. His book *The All-Weather Retirement Portfolio: Your post-retirement guide to a worry-free income for life* provides time-tested guidance for financial peace of mind, while *One More Step: The 638 Best Quotes for the Runner* inspires runners and others to realize their goals. His articles have appeared in *CPAFocus, Medical Economics Magazine, NW Style Magazine, 405 Magazine, Metro Journal, The Oklahoman*, and others. He is much sought after as a speaker for conferences, workshops, and broadcast media, including appearances on Fox News Network's *Fox on Money* and as the former host of the weekly radio program *Money Talks*.

Randy is also active as a volunteer in his community, and in 2005 received the Oklahoma Society of CPAs' Public Service Award. He is a member of the South Oklahoma City Rotary Club and sits on the boards, or is a trustee, of seven nonprofit organizations, including the Oklahoma State University Board of Governors, the YMCA of Greater Oklahoma City, the Oklahoma City Community College Foundation, and the Oklahoma City Employee Retirement System.

Most importantly, Randy is a family man who treasures time with his wife and son. He's an active member of his church community and an enthusiastic reader, writer, and runner.

For more information about Randy L. Thurman's work, and to contact him, visit his website at www.RandyThurman.com.

Index

cash, 47, 89-90, 100-101, 105, 154, 161-162, 215
stocks/equities, 28, 94-97, 101-102, 107, 117-119, 123-125, 129, 135, 143, 154, 186, 208-217, 239, 249

L

Leadership, 198

Liabilities, 5, 152-153, 155, 159-160, 162

Lifestyle, 4-5, 12, 32, 38, 190

Liquidity, 90-91

M

Matthews, Dr. Gail, 176

Mentor, 23, 129, 197

Morningstar, 119, 136

Mortgage, 5, 30, 41, 43, 45, 49, 52, 65-66, 70-71, 93, 162

Mother Theresa, 9

Murray, Nick, 129, 227

Mutual funds, 116-126, 135, 143, 154, 210-213, 226, 229, 249

N

National Credit Union Administration (NCUA), 105

Net worth, 5-6, 21
net worth statement, 151-156, 159-163, 250

P

Percentages, how to calculate, 70-71

Portfolio, 34, 89, 98, 100-101, 118, 123-125, 134, 136, 143-147, 183, 186-187, 207, 210-218, 226-227, 233, 236-239
More than a Millionaire portfolio, 213-216

Poverty, 9, 14

Priorities, 9, 11, 19-20, 22, 27, 62, 90, 147, 207, 222, 235

Profit, 93, 106, 129-130

Psychology, 38, 91, 174

R

Ratios, financial, 84-86, 157, 159-162

Rebalancing, 216-218, 226, 239

Robbins, Tony, 250

Roth IRA; *see Individual Retirement Account*

S

Seminars and workshops, 169, 172, 197-198, 245

Significance, 9

Spending plan, 42, 44, 46, 58-67, 76-83, 86, 152, 198, 202-203, 250
analyzing, 83-86, 160-162

Spiritual, 21, 24

Stocks; *see Investments, stocks/equities*

Made in the USA
San Bernardino, CA
06 August 2018